Elephant in the Room
Sex, the Gospel, & the Church

Dustin Hall

Remnant
Publications

Remnant Publications, Coldwater, MI

Published by
Remnant Publications
649 East Chicago Road
Coldwater MI 49036
800-423-1319
www.remnantpublications.com

Cover designed by David Berthiaume
Text designed by Greg Solie • Altamont Graphics

ISBN: 978-1-629130-13-2

Table of Contents

To my wife,

I tremble at the idea of being the kind of man described in this book. I commit to reflect and live out Jesus' love for you. Though I fall short in so many ways, it's what God promises to do in me; and it's what you deserve. You are a great wife and a wonderful mother.

—Dustin Hall

Introduction
The Elephant in the Room

There (in the hereafter) the loves and sympathies that God has planted in the soul will find truest and sweetest exercise.[1]

—Ellen White

"We also have the prophetic word made more sure, which you do well to heed as a light that shines in a dark place, until the day dawns and the morning star rises in your hearts." —2 Peter 1:19

The elephant in the room is the thing everyone knows is there but no one is ready to talk about. The obvious truth is being ignored or going unaddressed.

"Do you see it there … in the corner? Quick! Look, but don't let anyone see you're looking. Wait! Don't mention it either … no one talks about him … we don't know why, but it's just the way things have always been done. OK, so now you know he's there…just watch out for him … he's a little dirty. Don't get any of his diseases … and don't let him touch you or you might become impure! Oh, and some people think it's a sin but aren't really sure why. Remember, mum's the word."

There the elephant stands, unmentioned. Maybe that "elephant" has memories— pain, unanswered questions, or guilt attached to it. All turn a blind eye, yet there it stands, not as some innocent creature minding his own business, but as a voracious monster engulfing teens, married couples and anyone else who gets too close; and no one speaks up. His enormous growing mass causes great pain, leaves traumatizing memories and questions, triggers abuse, and pushes people out of the door never to return. Yet still he goes unannounced, and unchallenged.

In case you haven't noticed, sexuality is a dominant force in today's society. It pervades all media: TV shows, websites, magazines, billboards, personal text messages, e-mails, even political debates. So penetrating is its influence, it even invades personal thoughts. At the doors of the church however, there stands a kryptonite-like force field so strong that

---

1   White, Ellen. *Education*. Nampa Idaho: Pacific Press, 1903. 306.

no sexual content or thought must ever enter her doors. This last fallacy about the church is a grave one; for every person walks through her doors with some baggage. Whether it be impure thoughts, pain from past relationships, childhood abuse, pornography addiction, guilt from recent encounters, marital issues, STDs, lust for the person sitting next to them on the pew, or thousands of questions that they long to have answered by God. Clearly, the church is not impervious to sexuality. I personally know this to be true because, for the better part of the last 10 years, this is the prevailing topic for which people have sought my counsel.

It is a privilege to be part of the Church with the distinct knowledge of the Great Controversy between good and evil. We must however, avoid being devoured and acknowledge the growing presence of the elephant in the room. Sexuality is a critical battle in the war between good and evil, and we must take action.

What you are reading is both a wake-up call and a form of training. For nearly ten years I have been presenting biblical sexuality to both Christian and secular audiences. Without a doubt I can state that there is a problem with sexuality in our world. Romance and sexuality have become a false gospel of salvation, which I will explain in chapter one. The most concerning thing about all of this is that when it comes to sexuality, the youth of the world seem a bit better off in many ways; not because they are making better decisions, but because—as countless Christian youth tell me—there is no one they can trust who will talk to them about sex and personal issues. Worldly kids seem to have people they can reach out to, such as teachers, friends, parents or anyone else. Don't get me wrong, most often they are given terrible advice, but at least they have someone to talk to. An ironic and alarming fact is that there seems to be nearly as much sexual promiscuity among the youth within our church as there is outside it. Porn and sexual abuse are just as bad in the church, yet no one is talking about any of it.

At my seminars, when asked if they have ever heard a message about biblical sexuality in church, it is consistently only about one tenth of the youth that raise their hands. Of those who raised their hands, only three or four say it was a Christ-centered and inspiring message. The students who keep their hands raised report to me that the resources they have used are from evangelical Christian sources. Some of these resources are very solid, but it is long overdue that our church began to teach biblical sexuality from the perspective of Bible prophecy and the Great Controversy. Without that theme, a major piece of the puzzle is missing. Sexual purity and marriage are about the character of God. It is time that the church with the vital end time message began to uplift Jesus in the area of biblical sexuality within the Loud Cry. The book you hold in your hands is most of what I have learned presenting biblical sexuality for nearly ten years. I have found that all the answers about this crucial issue come back to Jesus, as they should.

The last observation I have is that you should prepare for what you are about to read: you may be a parent, pastor, or youth leader and should be ready for what you will encounter. As I present this material it convicts *me* of *my* own sins. To present it and study it I have to come to terms with impurity in myself. I wouldn't even be able to count the number of parents who have been sitting in the back listening as their kids answer an altar call, with tears in their eyes, realizing their own need to accept Jesus and His plan for biblical sexuality. There are also many parents who have asked me to help them understand how they can talk to their kids when they have made horrible decisions themselves. If you read this book, you will have to be convicted of sins and impurities in your own life. In fact, maybe that's why you're reading this book. If so, praise God. In order to truly know purity, we will be convicted of our own impurity. Please read this book prayerfully. With all of my heart I am convinced that we will lose an entire generation of our youth if we don't start presenting Christ-centered biblical sexuality in our churches on a regular basis. God, I believe, has called us to share Jesus through the message of sexual purity. It's obvious the devil is taking our youth away because of it. It's time we fight back! I hope this book is the beginning of this process in your church and in your home. If you are looking for very practical answers to common questions that young people have about relationships, my book: *Love's Lies God's Replies* is an excellent resource. If you are looking for a resource about understanding and teaching basic biblical sexuality, my book: *The Gospel of Sex* has helped many youth and parents.

This Book Is Written For:

▶ People who want to understand how the struggle for biblical sexuality is part of Bible prophecy.

▶ Young Adults who want to understand what true love is.

▶ The church; that it may know Satan's diabolical plan to destroy the image we see of the character of God through sexuality.

- ► Every person who wants to know and accept God's plan for biblical sexuality.

- ► Parents and Youth Leaders who want to finally speak up and be leaders in this area.

- ► People who are struggling to understand biblical purity, or have porn or relationship addictions.

Chapter 1
Sexy Beast

A god to replace the true God
A christ to replace the true Christ
Another gospel to replace the real Gospel
A love to replace true love
A way to get to heaven without the Savior from Heaven
Obedience to passions, not obedience to control passions
Worship to a god without worshipping *the* God.
False religion
False Reality
False Security
Worship of desire
Worship of self
Imminent destruction
An anti-christ: An alternative savior
A False Gospel

It has billions of disciples ...

> "I have been astonished that men could die martyrs for their
> religion—I have shuddered at it.
> I shudder no more.
> I could be martyred for my religion.
> Love is my religion,
> And I could die for that.
> I could die for you."[2]

—John Keats

2   Keats, John. *Bright Star: Love Letters and Poems of John Keats to Fanny Brawne*. New York, NY: Penguin Books, 1903. 72.

"The best love is the kind that awakens the soul; that makes us reach for more, that plants the fire in our hearts and brings peace to our minds. That's what I hope to give you forever."
—Nicholas Sparks, *The Notebook* [3]

"The madness of love is the greatest of heaven's blessings." [4]
—Plato

"I love you with all of my heart, body, and soul. You complete me. You make my life worth living. To have known you and to have loved you has been the most beautiful dream. I can only hope that I never wake up."
—Unknown

"Other men said they have seen angels,
But I have seen thee,
and thou art enough." [5]
—G. Moore

"The moment just felt right, like there was some force willing us together. So we did *it*. It was natural. We certainly have found our soul mates in each other. Now that I have her I feel like I can really see, like I really understand the things I was always meant to know. In her face I see the face of God."
—Testimony of too many of us.

"I use porn to feel alive."
—A 45-year-old man at one of my seminars.

"Blake said that the body was the soul's prison unless the five senses are fully developed and open. He considered the senses the 'windows of the soul'. When sex involves all the senses intensely it can be like a mystical experience." [6]
—Jim Morrison

3   Sparks, Nicholas, dir. *The Notebook*. Dir. Cassavetes Leven. New Line Cinemas, 1996. Film. 3 Oct 2013.

4   Norton, David. *Philosophies of Love*. Newark, NJ: Helix Books, 1971. 117. Print.

5   "http://en.wikiquote.org/wiki/George_Moore_(novelist)." *www.wikiquote.com*. Wikipedia the Free Encyclopedia, 03 10 2013. Web. 3 Oct 2013.

6   Morrison, Jim. "http://www.brainyquote.com/quotes/quotes/j/jimmorriso109335.html." *Brainy Quote*. Brainy Media, 17 9 2013. Web. 3 Oct 2013.

"I just felt that if I could find myself in the arms of the right man, that all of my pain from the sexual abuse in my childhood would go away."

—22 Year old female from one of my seminars.

Our hearts are being drawn to a magnet. They have been designed to be drawn to one source, one place, and one person. It's not who you think. Most people think it's their soul mate—or at least their one true love—but the Bible says something much different:

"The LORD has appeared of old unto me, *saying*, 'Yes, I have loved you with an everlasting love; Therefore with lovingkindness I have drawn you.'" —Jeremiah 31:3 (emphasis supplied)

---

hat's right; most people think it is another human being that is the one that we are being drawn to. They think that by finding "the one" they will be utterly happy and content, that in this person they will find peace. They believe that in sexuality they will find their true selves; that their identity is wrapped up in their passion and expression of that passion. People everywhere believe that sexuality will open the windows of life to its fullest, like a gateway to the eternal. Millions of teens believe that true love means it will free them from the bondage of a single life. The gospel of romance teaches that there is an inner self, something that resembles a soul that directs the physical nature of a person through love and sexuality to find the matching soul that will complete theirs.

The only One that can make us truly happy and give us true peace is God. Jesus is, after all, the Prince of Peace.

"You will keep *him* in perfect peace, *whose* mind *is* stayed *on You*, because he trusts in You." —Isiah 26:3 (emphasis supplied)

Everyone is trying to get back to Eden. Many people think they can do it by finding their Adam or Eve; but the only way to really get back to Eden is through Jesus. He is The Christ. He is the anointed one because He was the Son of Man who would come as God and Man to show us all what we really long for—Emmanuel, God with us. We are being drawn enduringly to the face of Jesus so that we might be saved. God through Jesus is pulling everyone to His side, the One Source of salvation. Any other perceived path to peace and love is another gospel, an anti-Christ message.

I would like to identify one anti-Christ for you. His name is Cupid. The word anti-christ literally means "in place of Christ." Satan has been able to replace the true Gospel with a false one. Over 70% of people in this country believe that there is one special person hand-picked for them that will bring them true peace. Over 80% of people under the age of thirty believe this[7]. Thus, a growing number of people believe that anything done in the name of finding true love and romance is totally acceptable, based on the fact that this is the only thing that could make them truly happy. That if only Cupid's arrow would pierce the object of their desire for them they could really start living. Most people think that something that is anti-christ is ugly and detestable, yet the gospel of sexuality and romance appears like the most beautiful and pleasing reality that has ever been. In fact, for many it is the *only* reality. People believe that the love that two humans can share heals all wounds and truly makes all wrongs right.

Take for example the quote above from the woman who had suffered sexual abuse. She believed that being sexual,and having relationships could heal her pain.

Only Jesus can do that.

G. Moore believed that the pursuit of divinity is all-encompassed by romance.

Jesus is the way, the truth, and the life.

The quote from the unknown source stated the commonly held belief that a lover makes life worth living.

Jesus is the light, and that light, the life of men.

Plato stated that love is madness and a gift from heaven. People cherish love-sickness.

Jesus said that he wants to give us a "sound mind" (2 Timothy 1:7).

Nicholas Sparks in the *Notebook* wants us to believe that it is romance that awakens the soul.

Jesus said that He is the one that makes us free and free indeed (John 8:36).

Satan doesn't care which anti-Christ you follow. The Bible says that many anti-christs would come (1 John 2:18). Whether you follow the Anti-Christ of Bible prophecy that Martin Luther, Calvin, Wesley, and Cotton Mather believed in, or another beast, it makes no difference to Lucifer.

---

7   Marist, Poll. "Most American Believe in Soul Mates." *Pebbles and Pundits*. Marist Poll, 10 2 2013. Web. 3 Oct. 2013.

He just wants you to follow a false gospel. *Any* false gospel at its foundation is a belief that somehow mankind can get back to eternity through some humanly manufactured system. The Biblical books of Daniel and Revelation reveal a worldly religious system that is the figure head for that kind of self made salvation, but make no mistake, there are many powerful anti-christ messages. They come in many forms, but all come back to one deception, that man can bring himself peace, that there is something in the human experience that can manufacture eternity for us.

Yet what false gospel could be more pleasing, attractive, and provide more immediate gratification than one based on love, sex, pleasure, passion, and romance? Beauty can be a corrupting influence. This is what the Bible says about Lucifer himself, "you corrupted your wisdom for the sake of your splendor" (Ezekiel 28:17 ESV). [8]

It is no wonder then that *true* love is under attack. 1 John 4:8 says that God is love. So if the Devil can make you believe a lie about love (God's character). He can make you believe a false gospel. And what a "sexy beast" he has created. He takes romance and love—a powerful and incredible gift given in Eden, something hand designed by God for worship to Him and discovery of Him—and makes it the most alluring, false gospel imaginable. The even more terrifying thing is that this message is so powerful we often shudder thinking of how to expose it. We are terrified to challenge it in our homes, with our kids, and in our church. Many pulpits are filled with messages about exposing false doctrine; but few pulpits ever present the explosive effects of a mind overtaken by the sexual gospel.

The most beautiful things are the most vulnerable things. Just ask Lucifer. It was his beauty that made him fall into sin (Ezekiel 28:17). It's not that love is ugly or horrible, in fact it's the opposite, it's a gift from Heaven bestowed with power and glory when it is done God's way. It is this power and glory that makes it vulnerable. It gives man a vague reminder of a long lost Eden. Using that longing, Lucifer convinces us that a romantic connection can take us back to that place. What man has overlooked is that the One who made Eden, and Eden's marriage—perfection, was Jesus. He created it. It was not Adam and Eve's love for one another that somehow spawned a garden. After all, first there was a garden, then there was a man, and then there was a woman and the gift of marriage and sex. It was Jesus' presence and His image in man that allowed Adam and Eve to love each other so unselfishly. This craving for Eden deep within all

---

8   The English Standard Version Bible. New York: Oxford University Press, 2009. Print.

of us is used by Satan himself to create a deceptive form of self-worship. We believe we may create in our lives an "Eden restored" by satisfying our passions in love and lust. In fact, this is the very opposite of true love. True love is other-centered, not self-centered. Lucifer has tricked us into falling in love with "love"; the worship of our own passion and desperation.

How many people have perished in the desert of loneliness while in pursuit of passion and romance? How many people have been led away from Christ because of a romantic relationship? How many people have destroyed their lives and the hearts of their families because they followed this false path to peace? How many young adults leave the church to find a spouse? How much sexual sin is committed to feel loved or appreciated for being convinced that the sexual gospel is the one that will save them? Millions of people are addicted to pornography because they can't find any other way to feel truly alive and satisfied.

People Believe:

- ▶ the theory that there is "hidden knowledge" to be discovered in true love.

- ▶ that in romance we become like gods; invincible, powerful, free, wise.

- ▶ that in romance there are no consequences; and even if there are, they are small in comparison to true love.

- ▶ that our very identity is defined by our feelings, and attractions.

- ▶ that satisfying our passions is the only source of peace. We are "sexual beings" after all, right?

- ▶ that absolute truth is only experienced within two people passionately loving one another, and anything that would limit this or restrict it, cannot be love. Because truth is based on every person's journey to be loved, there cannot be any absolute truth.

I have met many teens who believe that God honors their sexual activity before marriage because they are "in love" with someone that they are not in the position to marry. They have read all the Bible verses that deal with sex and they do not believe it applies to them. They believe that their "special" love trumps the context of those Bible passages.

They believe that true love conquers all.

Please look at the previous list of statements, and then compare them to the next paragraph taken from the book *The Great Controversy* in the chapter about *Spiritualism*.

> "Satan beguiles men now as he beguiled Eve in Eden by *flattery, by kindling a desire to obtain forbidden knowledge,* by *exciting ambition for self-exaltation.* It was cherishing these evils that caused his fall, and through them he aims to compass the ruin of men. "*Ye shall be as gods,*" he declares, "knowing good and evil." Genesis 3:5. Spiritualism teaches "*that man is the creature of progression; that it is his destiny from his birth to progress, even to eternity,* toward the Godhead." And again: "*Each mind will judge itself and not another.*" "The judgment will be right, because it is the judgment of self. ... The throne is within you." Said a spiritualistic teacher—as the "spiritual consciousness" awoke within him—"My fellow men, all were unfallen demigods." And another declares: "*Any just and perfect being is Christ.*" [9]

Is it possible that we have been so ambushed by the sexy beast and a false gospel that we have bought into a form of spiritualism? If so, we have believed that there is within us a way to heaven that does not include Jesus Christ, that somehow there is within us a divinity that is made manifest through sexuality.

This is one of the greatest battles the church has faced in this generation. The battle over true love and biblical sexuality is raging in our churches, in our homes, and in our minds. It is time that we had a reformation. It is time that we stopped being ashamed of it and allow Jesus to purify our minds (and our past if need be).

We must give a loud cry. There is already a false gospel in our midst—a sexual gospel—and too many of us and our children believe it. We must take down the sexy beast. We must allow the Holy Spirit to give it a deadly wound that will not heal. We must tell everyone that what they are craving is actually true peace and contentment in Jesus Christ.

---

9   White, Ellen. *The Great Controversy.* Nampa Idaho: Pacific Press, 1858. 554. Print.

Chapter 2
The Problem With Purity

I was recently reading an article written by a very agenda-driven blogger. The blog told the story of Elizabeth Smart, the young lady who was abducted, imprisoned, and abused sexually for almost a year. In retelling her story, Smart confessed that as she was being abused, she felt trapped by her abductor and never tried to leave because he had taken her purity. [10] As she thought about all her abductor had taken from her, one illustration used in her childhood church stuck out in her mind. Years before, her Bible school teacher had taken a stick of gum and given it to a student to chew for a few seconds. Then the teacher asked the student to take the gum out of her mouth and hold it up for the class to see. The teacher proceeded to tell the class that this piece of gum is what a woman is like once she has given away her purity. The blogger went on to make the case that this is the way all churches teach abstinence and purity. Later that day another young lady I was talking to—who had grown up in a different denomination than Smart—said that in a very real way, her value as a woman was tied to her purity and sexuality. If she had gotten pregnant, her family would have disowned her. They had taught her that her value to her future husband was directly connected to her virginity. She too was opposed to 'abstinence education'.

As I engage in these sorts of discussions I often get a bit of righteous indignation because these messages go against everything I believe and teach. When great generalizations are made about abstinence education—or 'purity educators', as some like to put it—I tend to get a bit defensive. Then, as I thought about it more, I realized they were personal testimonies from people who had actually experienced this kind of education. These things had actually happened to these people. Obviously people are being given a non-biblical view of God's plan for sexual purity.

---

10   Salzillo, Leslie. "Elizabeth Smart Says 'Shame from Rape' Kept Her from Fleeing Her Kidnapper." *Daily Kos.* Daily Kos, 07 05 2013. Web. 17 Oct. 2013. <. http://www.dailykos.com/story/2013/05/07/1207397/ >.

Women are being taught something that makes them believe they have no worth apart from their sexuality.

Others, like me growing up, never heard a message about it at all. Neither approach is helping young people navigate their lives and make good choices about sex. An illustration, like the chewed-up gum, is neither beautiful nor inspiring. It is in fact disgusting and further from the Gospel than what I can describe here. I believe that biblical sexuality is a piece of the Protestant Reformation that we have not yet fully come to terms with. God desires our purity, not for us to manufacture our worth, but because He has placed great value on our lives. Our choices about sexuality reveal our devotion to Him and the great plan of Salvation.

The idea that a woman's worth as a person and to God is tied into her virginity at marriage comes into Christianity from an interesting source— The Catholic Church. The church teaches of the Virgin Mary's purity her entire life. This purity was passed to Christ as her son. The virginity and purity of Mary is believed to be Holy and taught to the young ladies of the church. This ideology was greatly propagated during the reign of the church before and during the thirteenth century. The church had control of the arts, literature, philosophy and religion. In fact for many years, much of the romantic literature controlled by the church was swollen with Marianism. Today, much of the church, both Protestant and Catholic, are still influenced by the church of those days.

Is there sexual sin? Yes. Do people make mistakes? Yes. Do they need to ask for forgiveness? Yes. But from my experience let me share with you why this belief is so dangerous in trying to help people deal with sexual sin.

Sex is a physical, emotional, and spiritual act. When people engage in sex they share their bodies, minds, and hearts. Now, for a moment think about a so-called different kind of sin. Let's say without thinking and out of frustration and fatigue, I speak harshly to my wife. I used my mind for a moment. I spoke a word for a moment. I can very quickly make the wrong right with God and her by asking forgiveness. It was a simple mistake and easily forgotten.

What about sex? Can you make that wrong right so quickly? Can you take back the intense physical and spiritual influence of a sexual encounter? Can you take back all the feelings that led up to the event? Can you just change the fact that you are no longer a virgin? Can you just drop a relationship with someone that your body, brain chemistry, life, and emotions have bonded with? Can you just erase all the memories, addiction, and feelings, the brain has logged as a result of porn use? Can you just drop the feelings of hurt and pain that come from being abused? The answer to all these questions is, of course, no.

Now for a moment contrast the two realities: a church that is at best uncomfortable with sexual issues and at worst condemnatory, versus a loving boyfriend with a new baby, and perhaps, the adoration of friends and family. For others it may be the momentary gratification of sexual brain chemistry, or a secret no one knows of as you turn on your computer screen. It is much more appealing to deal with the guilt of living apart from the church and never telling them—or never going back—than to deal with a church that doesn't know how to treat the situation or is quick to make you feel condemned. You see, in many people's mind "purity" is closely associated with church. If a church does not present biblical and inspiring purity it will end up with a confused congregation. A confused congregation creates an uncomfortable atmosphere for a pregnant young lady, or an abused young man who already feels guilty. In this scenario "purity" is not very attractive. There is also the prevalent idea among many young people I have met who think that once you mess up you can never have purity again. Neither do they trust the people in their church enough to confess their sins and struggles. This sets many of our youth at odds with the church. They feel uncomfortable because they are living in sin, or are tempted by sexual sin and feel the church is either condemnatory or clueless, or both.

Another negative and often-used illustration to the youth involves a rose. A rose is taken from its wrapper—beautiful and perfect—by the teacher who then hands it to the students telling each touch it, look at it, and inspect its petals. As you may imagine, by the time this flower is paraded through the whole class it is in very rough shape. The teacher then holds it up for the whole class to see and likens the rose to what happens to their purity when they have sex outside of marriage. While the rose illustration might be a good visual aid to show what sin does in our lives, it also communicates a very negative message; for those who have made mistakes concerning sexual purity—you are like a beat up, worthless rose. Who wants a wilted rose? Now to be fair, what teachers are trying to do is show the effects of sin. Often they will raise up another perfect rose and explain the restoration Jesus can do in our lives. There is a serious flaw, however, with this illustration. Jesus is in the business of making wilted roses perfect again. Humans can't do this with a simple in-class illustration. So the message that ends up being communicated is that our worth is tied to our purity. So people who have messed up often don't want to talk with their teachers and identify themselves as the wilted rose. Who would?

I understand why some like to use visual aids like this. Those that have been brave enough to talk about sexual issues with their church youth groups want desperately to show them the gravity of their decisions. Sometimes we want to shock them in equal measure to the temptation, and powerful allure of sinful society. We want them to make the best decisions and show them something that will stick in their minds, but what ends up happening many times is that the message of love and hope we are trying to communicate doesn't stick. What sticks is a mental image of a wilted rose.

Let me give you a real life scenario that people ask me about often. A young lady in the church is dating a young man. Everybody knows that they are getting way too physical. No one says anything. The guy is not part of the church but comes occasionally. Guy and girl have their hands on each other way too much in church. It makes everyone uncomfortable. Everyone knows someone should say or do something but everyone looks at each other and ultimately says nothing, deciding "it's the pastor's job"; the pastor who has been there just a few years at most as opposed to the rest of the church who has seen this girl grow up from childhood. One day this girl stops coming to church. Now eyes start to roll, rumors start to swirl, a few people try to reach out to her but no one is really successful. After some time it turns out that one of the rumors is true—she is pregnant. Now there's a frenzy among the church to know what to do. Some say "drop her membership," others "we need to love her," others "we want to love her but not make it seem like we condone what she has done," still others, "I hope the pastor can figure something out."

Does this sound familiar? It probably has happened in your church or in a church you know about. I assume you probably cringed when you heard the illustration used by Elizabeth Smart's teacher. I wonder how many of you thought the person who said "drop her membership" had a point. You see both thoughts are one; that somehow sexual sin is more egregious than others. Is it? Is sexual sin worse than pride, anger, jealousy? Is any sin worse than another? There are some that live in open pride and others who are ashamed of sexual sin, yet it's the sexual sin that is often condemned. I seem to remember Jesus reaching his hand down to a prostitute inviting her to Himself with love. She didn't say a word, but He said "go and sin no more." Yet Bible scholars believe that that same woman still needed seven demons cast from her later in life (Luke 8)—the issue wasn't over, and still Jesus reached down for her. One of my favorite books *The Desire of Ages* talks about this very circumstance this way:

> "Mary had been looked upon as a great sinner, but Christ knew the circumstances that had shaped her life. He might have extinguished every spark of hope in her soul, but He did not. It was He who had lifted her from despair and ruin. Seven times she had heard His rebuke of the demons that controlled her heart and mind. She had heard His strong cries to the Father in her behalf. She knew how offensive sin is to His unsullied purity and, in His strength, had overcome.

> "When to human eyes her case appeared hopeless, Christ saw in Mary capabilities for good. He saw the better traits of her character. The plan of redemption has invested humanity with great possibilities, and in Mary these possibilities were to be realized. Through His grace she became a partaker of the divine nature; the one who had fallen, and whose mind had been a habitation of demons, was brought very near to the Saviour in fellowship and ministry." [11]

Did Jesus drop her name? Was her value to Him attached to her failures and impurities? Of course not; in fact I have found that many young people who are making sinful choices about sex are often longing to be delivered and offered a better way. Interestingly enough, being among the most hungry for victory and forgiveness, these never find the help they need from their own church. We as a church do a very good job of telling people about the Great Controversy, but we often do a terribly poor job of helping each other live through it. Yet as the body of Christ, that is exactly what we have been called to do.

> "But others save with fear, pulling them out of the fire, hating even the garment defiled by the flesh." —Jude 1:23

What if when that girl got pregnant, a lady from the church who she has known for years decided in her heart to redeem this soul for God? What if she started to visit with her? What if she helped her through the questions about pregnancy? What if she was there at the hospital when the baby was born? What if because Jesus loves this new baby, the church decided to love it too? What if this trusted lady from the church before or after the birth at the right time discussed her decisions, and because she

---

11   White, Ellen. *The Desire of Ages*. Namp, Idaho: Pacific Press, 2010. 568.

had loved this pregnant sinner, now she sees God's love acted out for her? What if this trusted church lady led this girl to ask for God's forgiveness?

What if these kinds of mentoring relationships started much earlier in life?

I suspect that most of us realize that sin is sin and God can forgive any sin. Not only does He forgive, He is the One who tells us we need to ask for forgiveness—which is proof He doesn't give up on us even when we make mistakes. When Adam and Eve sinned by eating the fruit, He didn't stay in heaven shaking his head at them, He ran to them searching, "Where are you?." Not because He didn't know where they were, but because He wanted them to know that He was right there looking for them.

Our value to Him is not wrapped up in our actions. Our value to Him comes solely because He loves us, and created us. He died to save us because He knew we couldn't work our way back to Him. He sweated great drops of blood in Gethsemane when willingly taking on the wrath of God because of our sins. Many of us know this, yet when it comes to sexuality, purity, and related issues we stand confused about God. Many are dumbfounded when it comes to issues like homosexuality, and other sexual topics. Is an acting homosexual any less loved by God? Is a Godly woman who has made mistakes in her past any less valuable to her church or her husband? We are living in the great controversy. Who hasn't been effected by the devices of Satan in one way or another? This is why the church exists—to help people overcome within the Great Controversy. We have been called together to overcome in Christ, no matter what our struggle is.

It is an interesting fact that the church squirms about sexual issues. From my experience, the reason we squirm is because few of us are free from some kind of sexual issue that's eating many of us alive—yet the church remains silent. These sexual issues are like a ticking time bomb if they go unaddressed. They blow up a marriage or a single person's emotions. As a pastor I have come to realize that it is the things we ourselves struggle with the most that we have the most difficult time dealing with in a Christ-like way.

We have to be brutally honest with ourselves for a moment. Is there a problem with purity in the church? I am saddened to say that most people would answer this question with an "I don't know." Yet, you are reading this book so you obviously are one who, at least, has some idea about this problem. The problem with purity in the church, as I see it, is far less about the "lust crazy people." Lust is just a part of the problem, but it's not the whole problem.

The greatest problem we face is that people believe a lie about what true love is.

Youth face challenges when it comes to waiting until after college to get married.

Husbands and wives are affected by the sexual baggage of the past or present.

People are having affairs.

We are letting our kids get into the dating culture.

Children are being abused at an alarming rate.

Satan keeps trying to shove his sexual and sinful agenda down our throats with media and peers.

The problem with purity in the church is that people are losing their sexual purity, and the church is not doing anything about it. Both sides of this equation are causing decay; the destruction of our young adults and others.

Let me share with you an experience I had recently. Over a period of one month I had the privilege to present my seminars to over 600 youth and young adults. During that time, fifty came to me personally to talk about problems they were having with pornography addiction. Many more asked me about how to end a physical relationship with someone they were not married to. As I spoke with these youth, some common themes kept resurfacing.

1. They knew what they were doing was wrong, but needed help.

2. There was no one they could trust in the church to speak to.

3. Because the church doesn't talk about these issues, they were beginning to rethink the validity of the Church's message. It seemed impractical and useless to them.

4. Many were using porn to self medicate deeper issues. The chemical concoction the brain puts out during porn use helped them overcome pain, depression, and anxiety.

I have read thousands of pages about how to keep the youth in the church, but if there were ever an outline of serious issues to address immediately it is the list that these youth kept revealing to me. We spend a lot of time talking about healthy living, but there is a message about health that is far more immediately serious than eating healthy food. It is the message of biblical sexuality. The greatest distress I have experienced as a pastor has been to see these young men and women—nervous, broken and scared—come to me with tears in their eyes because of the guilt in their hearts over what they are doing. They say that they haven't talked with anyone about it, feel trapped, and don't trust anyone in their church. The most eye-opening part of all of this is that they aren't youth we would consider "outsiders." Many of these young people are the leaders; the solid youth that are leading our youth groups. Another unnerving fact is that many have become so deceived about sexuality they literally believe God's laws about sexual purity do not apply to their situation.

If fifty of the leaders opened up about porn use over a one month period, how many more didn't, but should have? This tells me many of the statistics[12] I have seen are very plausible:

- ▶ Nine out of ten boys are exposed to porn before the age of eighteen.

- ▶ One out of every five mobile phone internet searches is for pornographic content.

- ▶ Fifty percent of men in the church report viewing porn on a regular basis and twenty percent of women

- ▶ One out of every five young adults report having made and sent at least one 'sext' (a text message with a picture of a sexual act).

According to the National Library of Medicine of the National Institutes of Health, Nearly eighty percent of collegiate young adults are engaged in sexual relationships outside of marriage. [13]

These statistics are not limited to non-Christians. This research doesn't discriminate. Some have even theorized that the use of pornography in the church is greater than that outside the church. In a later chapter we will discuss porn use and its effect on the life, mind and the church.

---

12   Covenant Eyes. "Porn Stats 2013." Covenant Eyes, 5 9 2013. Web. 3 Oct. 2013.

13   Bryant, KD. "Contraceptive Use and Attitudes Among Female College Students." *PubMed*. 20.1 (2009): n. page. Web. 3 Oct. 2013.

As I talk with hundreds of youth per year I get the increasing sense that I am the only person they have ever talked to about sexual issues. I very quickly begin to understand that they long to tell someone, but never felt like it was important or that someone could really help them. If they do talk about it, it's with a peer, or on the internet. An increasingly disturbing trend among teens is that they are much more likely to get their sex education from Google, than their parents.

To close out this chapter I want to tell you a true story. Eight years ago, when I first started going into public schools to talk about biblical sexuality, something happened to me that I will never forget. One day, after one of my classes, the middle school teacher pulled me aside after the students had left. The teacher went on to tell me that the previous day one of her students had come to her and told her that for the last five years a family member had been molesting her almost every night. After everyone in the house would go to sleep this family member would make his way to her room. Up until my presentation the previous day, she had never heard anyone tell her that there was anything wrong with that. She always felt it was disgusting and wrong, but didn't know how or why. She had prayed to God that it would stop, but it never did. She thought she just had to accept it, thinking it was natural. She had never heard anyone tell her ever before that it wasn't right for any man to treat her this way. She had never heard about setting boundaries, and how no person has the right to disobey God and trespass her personal boundaries without permission. That day was the first day she had asked for help because now she knew she needed it. She desperately wanted her feelings of guilt, pain and hatred to go away like we had talked about the day before and was reaching out to her teacher for help. I was stunned. I was twenty-four years old and not completely ready to deal with issues like this, but someone had to. God used me that day. He wants to use you and your church in the same way. It is an issue in *every* congregation in *every* part of the world.

I am convinced that sexuality is one of the greatest tests of our time. It is part of the Three Angel's messages in Revelation 14:6–12 because God designed love and sexuality to reveal His character. Just as the Three Angels proclaim to the world that God is love, we as a church should allow God to share this message in us to deal with the sinfulness in us and help real people like this young lady overcome the vicious plans of Satan. We have a problem with purity. The devil is trying his best to keep it from us and we are doing nothing to stop Him. The Devil is preaching a false gospel of romance and sexuality right under our nose and we are letting it happen.

Chapter 3
The Sexy Beast and Sexual Babylon

He had been lying to himself. His marriage of nearly ten years had lost that "spark." They had begun to argue, and he dreaded coming home most nights. While away on business trips, there was a coworker he just "clicked" with. They laughed at the same things and had the same talents. Soon he began to think he married the "wrong person." "If only" thoughts started filling his mind. One day, they shared a private dinner. She too had been having the same thoughts about him. It is interesting to note that this man had no idea he had been living a lie. As He was sharing this story with me, he only identified the ultimate act of physical adultery as wrong. He confessed when he was around the other woman (not his wife) he really felt alive and never realized the whole thought process prior to the physical act was just as sinful. This story is not unique and happens every day. It is happening in our own churches.

Are we really this messed up? Is it possible that we really have this many issues? Think about your life, your friends, and your family? How many sexual train wrecks can you think of? How many romantic mistakes that led to heartbreak and emotional baggage? Why do so many marriages have sexual issues? Why are so many men addicted to porn? Why do we invite into our lives so much sexual and emotional baggage? Is it solely our selfish hearts? Is it because we are helpless animals driven by lust? Are we responsible for our decisions? Yes. Is there also something much deeper and more complex at work? Without a doubt. I am convinced one of the greatest ways the devil does his evangelism is through lust and romance. He wants to draw our hearts to his ways by making us believe love is a lie and a lie is love.

God is love (1 John 4:8). Yet, when you hear the word "love" your mind almost immediately goes to a thought about romantic love between two lovers. Marriage, love and sex are very vulnerable to deception because of how beautiful and wonderful they were created to be. Love and romance are beautiful, and sexuality is a gift that was given to man to understand perfection (just read the Creation story). Yet the same devil who wants us to believe a lie about love (God's character) wants to deceive us about sex. In his fall he learned how to take the things that are most beautiful and make them vulnerable, selfish, and eventually sinful (see Ezekiel 28:12–18). He wants us to become so overwhelmed by the allure of the beauty of something that it no longer matters what context it is experienced in. Corrupted beauty quickly becomes selfishness. Selfishness causes an inability to see beauty in selfless true love.

In its proper context, attraction, love, romance, and sex are some of the most beautiful gifts God has designed for humanity. Out of its proper context however, it becomes dangerous and destructive. Ugliness alone is usually a weak temptation, but selfishness mingled with beauty and power result in an overwhelming deception. The church has largely had a hard time understanding how something so wonderful and full of passion and pleasure is properly understood. Some have refused to accept that God created it beautiful, or that man is so degraded that it is impossible to experience sex in a pure way. Others believe that since sex seems to be so overwhelmingly ingrained in man, that God accepts any behavior that satisfies a deeper journey to find ourselves through sexuality.

Because of the vast confusion about sex, over the years Satan has taken the beauty and power of love, marriage and sex and has used it to his advantage in the warfare over what people believe about God. "God is love," he whispers in our ears while we witness or experience lust, guilt, abuse, lack of self-control, betrayal, adultery, divorce, and teen pregnancies. Then he convinces us that the passing feelings, decisions and consequences that led to this pain were in fact God's fault and spins the saying to what he wants us to believe, "love is god." As a result, we have nearly a whole generation of people giving up on God, yet they still crave the unconditional love He is. Where do you think they run to find that love? They go to romance, sexuality, and a human mate. We believe love is god when the whole time we are craving Jesus Christ. We, too often, try to satisfy that desire with human relationships. The church has largely failed to communicate biblical sexuality in a Christ-centered way and as a result many young people today believe that the church's view on sexuality is obsolete.

We are often baffled over the decisions some young people make. They take enormous risks with their bodies, hearts, and futures over sex and relationships. At times it seems as though they are totally out of their minds. We will discuss brain development in a later chapter, but for now consider this: is it possible that because they have submitted to a lie about God's character, they are willing to take such enormous risks? I'm convinced lust is only a *part* of the problem, not the whole problem. Remember, God is love right? Or is love—god?

Love—Beauty or Beast?

A wealthy man lived in a mansion with his three daughters. One daughter was very pure in heart, innocent, and meek while the other two were very rude and proud. The merchant eventually lost all his money as the ships transporting a fortune of his merchandise overseas were lost in a storm. He was forced to sell all of his possessions and take his daughters to live in a small farmhouse in the country and work hard for their living.

One day the merchant heard that one of his ships had finally been recovered and quickly prepared to make a journey to the port to see if any of his merchandise had been saved. Before going, he asked his daughters if there was anything they would like him to bring back as a gift. The two selfish daughters asked for fine dresses and jewels, but the daughter who was meek and humble asked for a simple rose—a flower that wasn't native to their part of the country.

When he arrived, he learned his possessions were safe but had to be sold to pay his overwhelming debts. Depressed and crestfallen, the merchant began the walk home. After a long while he found himself lost in a thick grove. Hidden in this deep forest there was an immense palace. Hungry and tired the merchant decided to ask for refuge for the night. Upon entering the grand home, the merchant saw a huge table laden with food and drink—seemingly placed there for him by the home's owner who was nowhere to be found. The merchant stayed the night in the palace and rose early the next morning to depart. As he was leaving he walked through a rose garden and, remembering his daughter's request, plucked one of the roses for her. Upon plucking the rose, he was confronted by a hideous beast who was infuriated that, after accepting his hospitality, the merchant would take his most prized possession. The merchant pleaded for mercy stating he had only taken it for his youngest daughter, Belle. The beast agreed to let him go but only if he promised to return. The merchant was afraid, but accepted this condition. The beast sent him on his way, with jewels and fine clothes for his daughters but stressed that none of them—especially Belle who had asked for the rose—must ever know about his deal. After his return, Belle learned of her father's secret and decided to face the penalty for her father.

The beast accepted Belle willingly as she arrived at the mansion in place of her father. The beast crowned her the mistress of the castle. He dined with her every night engaging in conversation long into the early mornings. At the end of each of their nightly talks, the beast proposed marriage to her. She refused only to return to her quarters and dream of a handsome prince who would one day rescue her. Still, each night, the beast proposed marriage to Belle and she would in turn deny him; stating she only felt platonic love for him. She often would search the castle finding many enchanted rooms, but never the prince she longed for. Belle never thought that the prince and the beast could be the same person.

For many months Belle had the castle with all of its servants to cater to her every need, forgetting that she was a prisoner in the castle. The beast remained attentive and even showered her with gifts, but eventually Belle grew homesick and asked the beast if she may return for a visit. The beast granted her permission but only if she agreed to return in exactly one week. She walked home carrying an enchanted mirror that would allow her to see the beast back in the castle any time she gazed into it. After being home for a few days, Belle began to wonder about the beast. Looking through the mirror she saw the beast lying near his death inside the rose garden. She rushed back to his side and found that his illness was extreme heart-break. She cried over him; telling him that she loved him. As her tear trickled off her cheek and fell on his face, he was transformed into the handsome prince.

This story of course, is the famous *Beauty and the Beast* written by Villeneuve but later adapted and made famous in the 1700s by a woman named Beaumont. Is it a wonderful story about not judging a book by its cover? Or is it something more? We are told in the last days all the world will "wonder after the beast" (Revelation 13:3). Now why would anyone follow a beast? The biblical beast is after all a different kind of beast right? The beast from the story is lovely, and the beast from the Bible, sinful. Why would anyone choose sin? Sin is ugly, isn't it? Sin is murder, and hate, and selfishness, right? The story is beautiful but the Bible prophecy is ugly. Why would anyone love that? Why would anyone openly follow the devil? That would be foolishness.

Everyone wants to live forever. Everyone wants to live the most happy, contented life possible. Many realize that the Gospel is the only true source for happiness and fulfillment. However, as Paul warns in 2 Thessalonians 2:7, there will be false gospels that are spread by the "spirit of Anti-Christ." According to Paul, the same power that is behind the Anti-Christ of Daniel and Revelation also sends out other messages that are false Gospels leading people away from the true Christ. These messages would not be ugly. In fact, they would be seemingly beautiful—attractive.

What was it that changed the beast from the fairy tale, or did he change at all? Love shed Belle's tear. That "love" apparently turned a manipulative, selfish, terrifying beast into a prince. Don't forget that the beast was holding Belle against her will— she was a prisoner. Did the beast really change? Regardless of your opinion about the prince, the message in this story is that "love" was his savior. By making Belle fall in love with him, the beast saved himself.

- ► **Impatient**
- ► **Arbitrary**
- ► **Judgmental**
- ► **Selfish**
- ► **Megalomaniacal—delusions of power or omnipotence.**
- ► **Impassioned**
- ► **Nonsensical**
- ► **Critical**
- ► **Unreasonable**
- ► **Impractical**
- ► **Tyrannical**
- ► **Emotional**
- ► **Fickle**

What came to mind as you read this list? Some of you may have thought this was a list of lies people believe about God's character and reasons why they reject Him. Others may have thought of their love-sick teenage son or daughter and how much like these qualities they have become. So which is it? A list of beast-like qualities about the character of God that atheists claim, or a list of characteristics describing what people become when they listen to the lies of Satan about love?

- ► **Unconditional Love**
- ► **Eternal**
- ► **Gracious**
- ► **Patient**
- ► **Immutable**

- ► **Invincible**
- ► **Accepting**
- ► **Unchanging**
- ► **Reliable**
- ► **Trustworthy**
- ► **Wise**
- ► **Free**

What about this list? Is this list about God, or romance? Many people believe they achieve these things as they fall in love. Is it possible that the gospel of romance preached to us from the time we are young doesn't transform us into anything beautiful but in fact makes us more like the beast? Does this "love" make us like the first list; leading us to be self-deceived and making us more like Belle's captor?

Let's compare this idea to one of the most famous "love" stories of all time—*Romeo and Juliet*. Two families are rivals and hate each other. By chance, a young man from one family and a young lady from the other family meet and fall in love. They then scoff at the foolishness of their families, take enormous risks, betray their families, leave all they know for "true love." The play ends ironically with both young people committing suicide. They were willing to die because they could not be together.

Interestingly enough, we call this a love story while Shakespeare called it a tragedy. Was Shakespeare just another silly romance novel writer? Should the original copy of *Romeo and Juliet* have had a shirtless Fabio on the cover? Or was Shakespeare on to something deeper? Is the real lesson in *Romeo and Juliet* conveying that if you become intoxicated by a romance you think defines your life it will, in fact, end it? Which list from the two above do modern "Romeos" and "Juliets" think they are living out, the first or the second? I suspect that their thoughts tell them one thing, but their actions show something entirely different. The love that most people believe in and trust to make them complete actually is a gospel of self-satisfaction. Most people believe that by falling in love they will find true peace and happiness, and many are willing to do anything to feel that peace—or at least get what they think will put them at peace. This makes us much less like God and much more like a beast, yet it is this 'love' that the overwhelming majority spend their lives looking for. Its allure has destroyed many lives.

In ancient Greece, the famous doctor Hippocrates was the first to diagnose love sickness as a mental disorder. For over one thousand years doctors believed that love sickness would thicken and darken the blood, and if it lasted long enough would eventually shrivel the brain. While today love sickness is not diagnosed as a mental disorder, think for a moment about people in this condition who could be described that way. They display symptoms of sociopathic behavior, obsessive compulsive disorder, mania, psychopathology, eating disorders, and sleep disorders. Some become so addicted to love they start to behave much like a drug addict; only thinking and obsessing about his next fix. [14]

It is interesting how many fictional, fairy tale love stories end in death and even suicide. During the Enlightenment, when the Catholic Church had far less influence on literature, protagonists in love stories were glorified by suicide. In *The Sorrows of the Young Werther*, Goethe, a famous writer of that time, legitimizes suicide—which was formerly an ungodly and condemned act—by weaving a gorgeous love story with the suicide of a spurned lover—like a martyr to love. This was the first major story with such a theme.

Upon release of this book, there was a rash of suicides, some even very near to the author's home—as if he would understand their plight. These people believed if they couldn't have the satisfaction of their lover, life was not worth living. In the story, Werther commits suicide with a pistol after he is rejected by the woman he loved. Many men replicated this trend in an act of hopelessness. In that work the hero shoots himself after an ill-fated love, and shortly after its publication there were many reports of young men using the same method to commit suicide. [15] In another incident a young women drown herself behind Goethe's home with a copy of *Werther* in her pocket. She too had just experienced heartbreak.

Jeremiah 17:9 tells us that the heart is deceitful above all things and is desperately wicked. Yet our world tells us to follow our hearts. There is a reason why romance and sexuality are so intoxicating. We were made to crave the unconditional love of God; it's our gateway to worship. What Satan has done is create his own religion, his own worship. The god of that religion is romance, love, and sexuality. These are naturally endowed with supernatural blessings, but when taken out of their proper context, become selfishness. Every person wants to get back to Eden. The entirety

---

14   For more on this go to: http://abusesanctuary.blogspot.com/2009/02/romantic-sociopath. html. http://www.uwomj.com/wp-content/uploads/2013/06/v78n1.66-69.pdf.

15   Meyers, David G. (2009). *Social Psychology (10th Ed)*. New York: McGraw Hill.

of creation longs for that day. Marriage and sexuality were given in Eden. Romance has the power to take our minds back to what we were created for, yet it is not the plan that will ultimately take us there. So with these feelings, Satan tempts man to fixate on those fleeting moments of what we lost long ago. The sexual gospel teaches that the next lover, or the next porn flick, can give our minds the satisfaction and peace we all want so badly. It teaches us that to live without love is to not live at all, like the Beast dying by the roses. For many, losing love and losing life is the same thing. It is a false gospel. This deception is dangerous because it tells us that love is a lie and a lie is love and this is just what Satan wants. He gets to redefine love, and when we submit ourselves to that love he ultimately gets the worship. We are convinced the whole human project is a joint activity predicated on love and sexuality, which is true but, understood properly through the love of God for man. By believing the lie that sexuality and romance drives our existence, and not God's love for us, we are doomed to failure. Studies show that relationships based primarily on romance and sexuality end within seven years. And this is the "love" that many people compare God to.

Just listen to nearly every secular love song on the radio. Consider the cover of every romance novel. We are not drawn to sexual sin and impurity simply out of lust, we have been deceived to believe it is true worship to "the real" god taking us to where we were really meant to be.

Consider words from a famous song from the movie "Aladdin"—

> "I can show you the world … When was the last time you let your heart decide … A whole new world! A new fantastic point of view. I can open your eyes! Take you wonder by wonder … Indescribable feeling … No one to tell us 'no' or where to go, or say we're only dreaming … Amazing place I never knew … I'm in a whole new world with you." [16]

Did you catch the theme? Romantic love, and ultimately sex opens your eyes to a new reality. You have never lived, seen, felt, or heard it until you have surrendered to this love. In other words, you get a heaven-like experience as you fall into this love. Does this deception sound familiar? Long ago Satan whispered in a woman's ear to tell her very similar things (Genesis 3). Lucifer flattered Eve, made her think she was meant for a better, free and more empowered existence. All she had to do was eat that fruit and he would open her eyes.

---

16   Pebo Bryson, Regina Belle, *A Whole New World*. Aladdin Motion Picture Soundtrack. 1992.

Married people know well that you don't enter a whole new world on your wedding day. It's the same world, but with far more responsibilities. With more responsibility comes more stress, with more stress, more discontent. Then the doubt begins. "Have I not married my soul mate? Perhaps I haven't discovered true love? I can only be happy by finding true love."

This is the lie that many people believe. They pursue the false god of romance so fully that they often destroy their lives in the process. What they don't realize is that by running after what they believe to be true love they are actually running toward a vicious downward spiral of destructive selfishness. What we are talking about here is a religion with a false god. A god lying about offering salvation from a hopeless source.

If that didn't convince you, this might. These are the words of a hit song from 2013 by an artist named Bruno Mars—

> "Never had much faith in love or miracles … But swimming in your water is something spiritual … I'm born again every time I spend the night … Cause your sex takes me to paradise … You make me feel like I been locked out of Heaven for too long … you bring me to my knees, you make me testify … You can make a sinner change his ways … Cause your sex takes me to paradise … [17]

A Whole New World is a song that is at least twenty years old. This last one is contemporary. One targets kids and the other—adults but the message is the same: sex and love are a religion that will bring you true knowledge and salvation. Now think back to all the romantic comedies, all the romance novels, all the TV shows you have seen, even all the "oldies" on the radio about love … isn't the message the same (think *Earth Angel*, and *Can't Help Falling In Love With You*)? It's the theme of movies like *The Notebook*, and *Titanic*. The most dangerous thing is that the media isn't putting foolish, unbelievable material out there—no one would watch or listen to it. They're offering something that deep in our sinful hearts we already are prone to surrender to. It's powerful propaganda for an ultimate deception. Close observation of current culture reveals most people reject the most unbelievable parts of media (zombies, and vampires), but accept the underlying love stories and elements of romance that seem to resonate with them.

---

17   Bruno Mars. *Locked Out of Heaven*, Unorthodox Jukebox. Atlantic Records. 2012.

Is it really that far-fetched to believe there are strong spiritual connections to love, romance, and sexuality? After all God gave it to Adam and Eve in perfection. Just like He made Lucifer perfect and beautiful in all his ways, He made sexuality. Lucifer's beauty was a gift from God to show His unselfish glory, as well as with sex. Yet something that was created to show God's glory people now use to worship self, and not God.

The devil has succeeded in his plan to blame God for all of the hateful things mankind is becoming, and make them think they can rise to a higher level as they discover love, romance, and sex. We have been deceived into thinking that if we are not in love, or feeling loved, or being worshipped by someone, or having sex with someone, we are somehow missing out on true reality. We are led to believe that human love is an oasis of salvation in this world.

If a girl's prince charming hasn't come, she believes she must be doing something wrong, or she isn't beautiful enough. If that guy hasn't dated a certain amount of gals by a certain age he believes that he must not be "manly enough." If a person is confused about certain feelings with their sexuality they must not have found their true identity yet. In fact, love and sex have even become a sort of creator in the minds of many. Think about it… in our culture, is sexuality looked at as a gift or the *definition* of who you are? Is it cherished as a holy thing created with Godly power? Or is it simply part of our base, human, animalistic foundations? Are we sexual beings or children of God? Does your sexual attraction make you who you are?

I was once talking with a sex educator who did not share the same views about sexuality that I have. She believed that any suppression of sexual urges actually harms the psychology of a person, (by the way this is a major theory among prominent sex educators). This was an educator who was given the opportunity to teach a group of middle school students a few weeks before I was able to present to that same group. This kind of education also represents the belief of a large segment of our society. This view gains hundreds of millions of dollars in funding every year from our government. Is it any wonder that we have children as young as eight and ten years old experimenting with sex? Is it any wonder that pornography addiction has been reported in children who are as young as eight to twelve?

Sex as an identity … sex as a god … sex as a personal discovery of your human nature … sex as your savior.

30% of people 18–29 report that they are religiously unaffiliated. [18]

I beg to differ, because everyone worships something; it may be a career, or it may be sex. It's easy to see that the porn industry is a multi-billion (yes, that's with a "b") dollar industry. Romance films and romantic comedies continue to stream from Hollywood. People continue to reason that their marriage could not continue because they "fell out of love." The TV shows and movies that have the most sexual content are actually written specifically for the 14–25 year old age group. Is it possible that the reason we are losing this age group in our church is because they have given up on Christ and taken up the message of the Sexy Beast and his false gospel of pleasure and self-seeking? The anti-Christ message teaches us that true religion is self-pleasing; it's not transformative but actually accentuates who we really are.

The devil has made us believe that true reality and true living are tied directly to sexuality; that the way to really live is to date more, flirt more, have more sexual partners in order to find true love and your true self. And when true love is found you will be living in "A Whole New World"; free to experience life the proper way. If you ever feel that you are not living in that "whole new world" any more feel free to do whatever it takes to rediscover that "whole new world" again.

I am convinced that part of God's call to His people in the last days is to "Come out of Babylon" (Revelation 18:4). Babylon is a symbol for confusion; a state of confusion about God, His character, and true worship.

Are people really finding what they are looking for and what they are convinced they will find in romantic relationships?

Studies show that substance abuse and depression are closely related to promiscuity. [19]

One of four people in the US will contract an STD at some point in their lives. [20]

---

18   Stetzer, Ed. "Morning Roundup." *Christianity Today*. Christianity Today Magazine online. http://www.christianitytoday.com/edstetzer/2013/march/morning-roundup-031413-new-atheism-is-dead-trends-in.html Oct 2013.

19   Ramracka, S. "The relationship between multiple sex partners and anxiety, depression, and substance dependence disorders: a cohort study ." *PubMed.* 42.5 (2013): n. page. Web. 3 Oct. 2013.

20   Planned Parenthood of Western NY, . "1 in 4 Americans Has STD." *Our Words Our Work.* 4 2009: 1. Print.

Four people for every thousand will be divorced this year alone.[21]

Here is the question: is our understanding about true love paying off? As our kids build emotional, sexual, and relational baggage for themselves are they really discovering rest for their souls like culture is telling them they will? We have seen this to be false. Many of us have experienced the same empty feelings they have or will. If there has been an attack on romance and true love, and the whole world has been deceived by the devil's lies, perhaps it's time we made an inspiring, biblical message about true love as a main part of our encouragement as parents. Isn't it time to make Godly sexuality part of the message we teach and preach at church? If so many are being led away from God because of sex and relationships perhaps we should teach about the God of truly beautiful sexuality and what true romance is really about.

Long ago many people, through temptation, decided to seek safety and show their prominence by building a huge tower. The destruction of Noah's flood was still on their minds and doubt about God's promises to never destroy them again overcame them. Because they thought they knew what was wise and right, they began to build this enormous structure. This tower would reach into heaven. This tower was a symbol of their wisdom, achievement, and safety. God had to remind them of their total reliance on Him. He came down and destroyed the tower, and dispersed man over the Earth by establishing different languages for humanity. Today one very dangerous Babel-like tower—among many others of man's creations—is love and romance. Interestingly enough when disaster does come to our love lives all we tend to do is blame God and keep looking for romance, when we really should remember our dependence on Him. Jesus is true love. He is our all in all. He is our salvation. The only way for us to drop the baggage, to feel content, to find rest for our souls is to feel loved in Him. No person or romance, or sexual experience can ever fill the cross-shaped void in our hearts. It's time we came out of the Babylon of sexuality. It's time we helped our youth stay out too.

---

21   http://www.cdc.gov/nchs/fastats/divorce.htm April 24.2013

Chapter 4
Out of Sexual Babylon

There are many Christians who attempt to present biblical sexuality. Many books have been written. Very recently I looked at the website of a well-known Christian publisher and it stated that they are no longer seeking manuscript submissions on relationships and sexuality; they feel they've published enough. There are many very good books and resources out there; however, of the many I have read, they missed out on one great and central biblical theme: the Great Controversy. The battle over love, sex, marriage and relationships is actually about the whole world seeing God for who He truly is, or being deceived by their choices about sex. This is a battle that is waged between good and evil over our minds and hearts.

In the last chapter we outlined this vital understanding. Now let's get a bit more practical with it. Without understanding purity in the context of the Great Controversy, most messages about sexuality come back to some basic arguments, and they sound like this:

▶ Save sex for marriage because you want to remain "pure."

▶ Save sex for marriage because you want to avoid getting pregnant.

▶ Save sex for marriage because you don't want to get a disease.

▶ Save sex for marriage because of your future.

▶ Save sex for marriage because you want to avoid sin.

In and of themselves these are very good in theory. All of these things we want to avoid, or apply. However, with every seminar I conduct I find our youth believe a "true love" experience trumps any of these possible consequences. In other words, they are willing to take the risks because they are in love with someone. Said more plainly, they don't even think sin is sin if they are in true love. If you look carefully, all of the above reasons to stay pure center around the person. They essentially leave God out of it. So youth and churches are left to decide what's best for them even if the reasons are biblical. This really doesn't help us overcome the real heart of the sexual purity struggle—selfish hearts. *Since sex is presented in the context of self, often selfishness wins out.* Many well-meaning abstinence educators use these arguments as the crux of their messages. I have taken some time to talk with youth who have sat through these types of seminars. Think through some of the real-life reasoning I have heard from them:

▸ If they get pregnant out of wedlock, it's no big deal; they'll be together forever anyway.

▸ If they get a disease, it's no big deal; they'll go to the doctor. If it's incurable it's a cross they are willing to bear to be with their soul mate.

And the most dangerous belief of all…

▸ It's not really sin because they are in "true" love. Marriage is merely a formality. What really matters is what is in the heart.

While many of the arguments purity presenters give are solid, they end up being too focused on human relationships and not on the human and God relationship. For some reason invincibility has been linked with sexuality. So teens and young adults consider consequences, yet often think they will not have an effect on them, or they believe true love will help them rise above any possible side effects. This type of education has actually been shown to work well in the temporary immediate context, but eventually breaks down especially during college.

I quickly learned this fact when I first began presenting to junior and senior high students. I had been using some curriculum I thought was excellent, from a non-denominational Christian source. This curriculum spent one whole class day presenting the effects and prevalence of STDs/ STIs. I'd stand there talking to them about the STD epidemic, giving them what I thought was staggering—overwhelming arguments about why they should save sex for marriage—and they would just stare at me, bored. In fact, the only real time they seemed to get interested was during an illustration with hydrogen peroxide and water that demonstrated how quickly a disease can spread if you have more than one partner. What I learned was that they were more interested in the novelty of the science project than they were with the lesson I was trying to teach.

Thinking back to the last chapter, let's make the comparison again; Satan makes a devilish transformation playing on our own selfishness taking sexuality from being a gift, to it being a sort of religion. Ironically, the risks people take regarding their love lives resemble the kind of service one gives to Christ in the Great Commission. Millions of youth everyday are willing to risk life and limb to achieve a human love—an attempt at unconditional selflessness—when the only true source of this kind love is Jesus. This deception is genius. Because of its immediate gratification, a life in pursuit of the "love god" is more immediately satisfying than the slow, patient work of the infinite God. *Interestingly enough, by giving all for love, most people are giving all for self.* It is the reward of romance that drives the pursuit of it. In this false religion, there are plenty of tracts to spread the message. There is plenty of media to drive home the point. There is even a church you can go to for encouragement—"friends."

What I learned very quickly ministering to teens is that they don't make difficult (but healthy) decisions because they are scared of the negative consequences of a bad one. One makes a good decision because of its result. One makes a good decision because what one is really looking for in human relationships, one can only find in Jesus.

Let's be very honest with ourselves for a moment. Which of the following messages create more immediate inspiration and are more attractive?

▶ "Here is the list of STDs and how gross they are. You could really easily get one of these."
vs.
"Find your real identity through sexual exploration and live life to its fullest."

▶ "God says sex outside marriage is a sin."
vs.
"We are in true love and we will get married someday anyway, but if we don't it was all really great while it lasted."

▶ "You will disappoint your parents."
vs.
"Sex with him just seems so right, and makes me feel really loved."

▶ "If you are not pure you could be eternally lost."
vs.
"True love is purity, so anything done in its pursuit is a pure action, no matter what context that action is done in."

A life headed for self-destruction just seemed a whole lot more attractive than an abstinent life of singleness didn't it? You see ... a person convinced against their will is of the same opinion still.

So, rather than listing all of the horrible things that come along with promiscuity, why don't we shift our focus? Rather than showing what STDs are and talking about teen pregnancy as an attempt at motivation, why not proclaim Jesus as the source of veritable true love? Comparing Christ to anything Satan could devise is a far better strategy. Exposing the lie about love, proclaiming the nature and character of true love, and showing how we are involved in that plan, in a real-life way, is far more convincing and inspiring than the current modus operandi. Think about it. Has anyone ever accepted Jesus by looking at pictures of gonorrhea? I would even submit that no one has ever accepted Jesus by looking at sin. There is nothing redeeming about sin. People accept Jesus by knowing and seeing Him for what He is, a Savior from sin.

Choosing purity is about choosing Jesus, not avoiding teen pregnancy. You don't help people spot a counterfeit by showing them counterfeit bills. You help them to know the real thing. When something dangerous or fake comes along it sticks out like a sore thumb—or a painful disease.

> "Christ calls upon the members of His church to cherish the true, genuine hope of the gospel. He points them upward, distinctly assuring them that the riches that endure are above, not below. Their hope is in heaven, not on the earth. 'Seek ye first the kingdom of God, and His righteousness,' He says; 'and all these things'—all that is essential for your good—'shall be added unto you.'"[22]

When I first got into teaching biblical sexuality, I thought the battle was simply about information, and conviction, people deciding to not act like animals. What I have learned over the years is that good biblical sexuality education is about truthful, spiritual, and healthful information, but more so about the core of sexuality and relationship. Every crying young lady who needs to talk, every young man struggling with porn, every young adult dating someone outside the church is looking to find something; true love. What most have never realized is that true love is not found, it is made. True love is about service and selflessness, yet the world around us tries to convince us that all love is and represents might be recognized and experienced in a moment; and that "moment of

22   White, Ellen. *Counsels on Stewardship*. Hagerstown MD: Ellen G. White Estate, 2010. p. 218.

fireworks" can last a lifetime. *True love is actually about many moments over the course of a lifetime.* Better said true love is eternal, not because it is any sort of passion that two human beings can enjoy between them, but because true love is Jesus. The greatest hurdle I have found in my ministry to young people choosing a biblical plan for true love is that they are looking for a love that doesn't exist. The greatest obstacle for people in achieving a truly successful plan for love is to realize that they are looking for unconditional love, contentment, and satisfaction from sources that can never provide it. Yet because this is the world we live in, these are the only sources they know.

I don't want to give you a script of what to say or think but I want to give you things to consider and wrestle with. This way, you can communicate God's will to the person, teen, or young adult you are speaking with. To call people out of sexual Babylon is to call them to know Jesus for what He is. This is a list and brief commentary on some of the things I have found helpful when asking people to choose Jesus' wonderful plan for their love lives. To really help people choose God's plan for love, they must choose Jesus; Real Love, really and truly.

1. **God is our Creator**—The One who can measure the universe with the span of His hand (Isaiah 40:12), strains His ear to listen for your voice as you worship Him (Psalm 147). If He is this in love with you, to block out all the praise from the whole universe to listen for you, he must have an amazing plan for your life. If you make choices that are out of the plan that God has set, you can prevent that amazing plan from moving on as He planned.

2. **God is Our Romance**—Every sunset, every opening flower, every shooting star, every bit of food on your plate, every time your mother says "I Love You," every miracle, every cool breeze on a hot summer day, every word of encouragement just when you needed it, every time your heart leaps for joy—this is God romancing your heart. If we expect a human being to fulfill what only God can, we will never feel really loved. He longs for you to realize that He is drawing, calling, and romancing your heart with its every beat. God literally works to earn our love.

3. **Jesus desires a powerful relationship with us**—Mankind chose to rip itself away from God. God knew we would try to do this so before He created us he made a decision to never be away from us. Jesus would come and die so that He could always be "God with us." He left perfection and came to this tiny planet just to have a chance to

be with you and me. Deep in our hearts we sense that someone is out there for us. We often think it's some soul mate, but it's not. It's Jesus calling to us from heaven, speaking to us from the cross, shouting to us from the empty tomb, and whispering to our longing hearts.

4. **God is Our Contentment**—Hebrews 4 calls Him our "rest," He promises to be our Rock, our fortress, our salvation, our Provider, powerful, all glorious, always watching us, gave his life for us, our shield, our strength, the Good Shepherd, the Bread of our life, the Light. No romance, no sexual experience can bring us the contentment that Jesus can. Many women run to men to feel safe and valued, men run to women to feel loved and appreciated. The problem is the contentment that human arms provide always fades quickly away. The only way to find a real genuine human romance is to first be content in the One who created you; to know Him who promises to provide every good thing.

5. **Identity is found in God**—We were created in His image. It is an amazing thought that the more we get to know Him, and live a life of worship, the more like ourselves we really become. God created this world to function perfectly. The laws He set up created perfection and freedom. When we choose to live outside that plan for life, it creates hardship and puts us in bondage. Sexual promiscuity, exploration and everything involved with it is an attempt to find "self" in something that was never designed for such a purpose. Sexuality is a gift to man, *not man's identity itself.* There is a person that God is trying to mold each one of us into. When we go to any other source to find that person it is a futile endeavor.

6. **Everything is Marriage Preparation.** God loves us enough to give us the freedom to choose. The choices you make today will determine the freedom of your future. God has given all of us the ability to choose self-control. We are not bound by our past, the way we were raised, or anything that has happened to us. We have the power, by God's grace, to determine what choices we make and the people we want to become. Jesus died to make it possible for us to be free from the bondage and baggage of sin, now the choice is ours as to what path we walk in life. Choices according to His plan lead us to achieving our goals and living the life God intended. The choices we make today affect our lives tomorrow.

7. **Love at First sight is often cured by a second look.** Who can really trust their emotions? Too often we are fooled by our hearts and

minds, but God's plan never fails. He is really the only good match-maker. Too many sexual and emotional mistakes are made by try-ing to follow our own plans. How many people get involved with each other romantically and sexually only to find out that they were sucked in too fast and really did not know the person they were involved with? Emotions change, the things we find attractive of-ten mature with us. To make life-altering decisions based on our hearts and feelings is a really dangerous thing. But there is a God in Heaven who created us to be at our happiest when we make deci-sions based on Him. Is our culture really happier when "following their hearts"? If God is love, then it's best to leave our love lives to Him to make beautiful.

8. **Sex is Worship**—God gave sex as a gift to human beings in the Garden of Eden. Everything in the garden was designed for rela-tionship, worship and discovery of God. Our society tells us that the hook-up culture, sex, and attraction are all to create satisfaction for us. God has shown us by giving us His Son that true love is service and selflessness. Sexuality was designed to be an intimate way for a husband and wife to communicate physically with one another, to create an emotional and physical bond, and to realize that peo-ple were created to feel the most content and satisfied when we are meeting the needs of another person. Individuals begin to respect sex when they understand that sex was not primarily created as a form of self-gratification, but for communication, discovery and in some way a reflection of God's connection within the Godhead. Now don't get the wrong idea, this is simply a human way to discover the intimacy of selflessness and the harmonious communication within the persons of the Godhead; not that God Himself is a sexual being. Helping people understand what sex was created for and the reason why it's such a special gift is an essential element to teaching purity. As this selflessness is expressed physically, it can also lead to another form of educational selfless service: raising children.

9. **Jesus shows us He is true love**—People more than ever are genu-inely looking to feel loved, appreciated, and desired unconditionally. Human beings in marriages and romances can never be that kind of love—even though Hollywood would have us believe it. Is there anything more that Jesus can do to show us that He is this very kind of love? By what he has done and is doing for us He is showing us our worth to Him, that He places infinite value on our lives, and that there is nothing that will ever separate us from that love.

10. **Jesus is making a marriage proposal to all of us**—Every moment of our lives God is showing that He is the ultimate bridegroom. He provides for us, takes care of us, saves us from danger, and looks out for our temporary and eternal welfare. He is asking for our devotion and our love in return. Is there any reason why we wouldn't accept His proposal? How do we show that we say "yes" to His proposal? Trusting that He really does have our best interests in mind with our obedience and submission to His will is our acceptance of His proposal; it is our fidelity to Him. As we obey Him, even when it is difficult, it builds our character and is like us keeping our wedding vows to Him. This choice allows Him to fill us with Himself through His spirit. Few of us consider that sex outside of marriage, pornography, and a desperate dependency on human romance is like committing adultery on God. It violates our commitment to Him. Our choices about sexuality are not just about us, they are also about us and God. Our choice about our sexuality has the opportunity to proclaim "Worthy is the lamb!"

This list is brief and incomplete but the rest of this book will take these themes and flesh them out in greater detail. My purpose in sharing this was to draw attention to wonderful truths about Jesus that apply directly to our romantic lives. The true way to help ourselves and our youth come out of sexual Babylon is not through scare tactics, or focusing solely on the effects of sin. After all, God's repeated message to us is, "Look to me and be saved, all the ends of the earth! For I am God, and there is no other" (Isaiah 45:22).

The way to help each other choose God's plan and overcome in the battle over sexual purity is to proclaim the matchless charms of Christ. Jesus is the fullness of love for man. Human romance is simply an expression and discovery of what He is for man Himself. Every one of us will struggle with sexual sin and temptation until we allow this truth to fill every corner of our hearts. The more of Him we have in our hearts, the better our marriage, and personal lives will be, and the more our love life will be full of true love. I believe some people who would like to be married and aren't, still wait because God is patiently teaching them this important truth before he shows them someone that is well suited for them. Some may even miss Godly people who God has brought into their lives because they have not learned this all-important truth. God cares about your love life because He, Himself is love. Any relationship that we enter into without fully understanding this leaves us vulnerable to discouragement, sin, and lies from Satan about God. Understanding that

Jesus is the true fulfillment of our hearts' longing even helps redefine attraction for us.

> "I have made a covenant with my eyes; Why then should I look upon a young woman?" —Job 31:1

For many, sexual attraction is believed to be a fulfillment of the inner desperate need of humans. The only way to make Job's kind of covenant with our eyes is to realize that even looking and lusting, and even sexual satisfaction is not what we really desire. It may be pleasing for the moment, but any deep desire for pleasure is actually a fallen human's innermost cry for the deepest fulfillment that only Jesus can satisfy. So the only way out of sexual Babylon is to gaze deeply at and grow to know intensely the Rose of Sharon—Jesus AKA True Love.

Chapter 5
Identity Crisis

"To be yourself in a world that is trying to make you something else is the greatest accomplishment." [23]

—Ralph Waldo Emerson

I remember a friend of mine who in high school thought he was the greatest basketball player to ever step onto a court. He began to take on the "jock" persona. He dressed like an athlete, went to all the "jock" parties, dated the "jock-group-approved girls" and pared his friendships down to only those who fit in with his jock worldview. My friend then graduated, and his basketball career came to an abrupt halt. He started hanging out with a girl who loved country music and he started listening to Tim McGraw. He bought a truck. He had never owned livestock or so much as set foot on a farm; nevertheless he started buying Wrangler Jeans and wearing cowboy hats. Then he went to college and took on his current persona: a school-teacher. This is a true story.

How do we come to know who we are? What are we supposed to look like, dress like? Who are we to make friends with? How are we to decide who we really are? This debate is especially raging in the discussion over sexuality and identity. There are new terms like "gender identity" where psychologists try to help people discover "who they really are" and if in fact the physical gender assigned to them at birth fits that identity. This idea is prevalent when considering gender confusion and people who believe they are transgender. This discussion is important because it plays a vital role when it comes to understanding the role of sexuality in life as human beings.

Another hotly contested argument is about sexuality and whether or not someone is genetically a homosexual or not. The truth is, this debate can

---

23   Emerson, Ralph Waldo. *The Essential Writings of Ralph Waldo Emerson*. New York, NY: Random House, 2000. 328. Print.

never be decided with science, because this issue deals with the very origin of man, and a supernatural warfare over the God given identity of mankind. This has in recent years created an even greater schism between many in the scientific perspectives of Darwinists and Creationists. This has become counter-productive; rather than letting science and scripture teach us more about ourselves, many are closing doors to understanding how God really made us, and what has happened to us since. Along with this debate, is another one raging among "sex educators." who say that sex is so deeply rooted in our nature that it defines who we are as a person. This view comes from Darwinism. Darwin believed that the sole purpose for an organism was to pass on his or her traits to the next generation, thus human sexuality became part of the process. Others frankly don't know how to reconcile the depth of sexuality in themselves and their experiences with the very weak arguments from a non-biblical standpoint that others create. Because of the lack of sound biblical teaching from churches, even many Bible believing Christians believe that men are defined by their success with women, and women are defined by their ability to bring in prince charming.

Far too many times I have heard fathers say of their sons, "…real ladies man, just like his dad." In the store you see girls' sweat pants with "sexy" written across the backside. To us sexuality is far more than just a label, it is an understanding of self. This is nothing new. Thousands of years ago civilizations like the ancient Egyptians adorned their women with makeup, jewelry, and sexually flattering clothes. Students of Darwin state that it is the very nature of men as animals themselves to mate with as many females as possible. To be promiscuous is part of natural selection. People everywhere believe that sexual expression is the very essence and purpose of a person. It has become a way of life.

One of the greatest questions mankind has asked for thousands of years is: how did God make us? More than ever before it is important for us to understand whether or not we are really just slaves to sexuality. Is "sexy" ingrained into our identity? Or is the gender and sexuality that God gave to man something beautiful, and part of how we understand ourselves but not the very definition of us as created human beings? What *is* the very definition of man?

I am not a neuroscientist. I have read many articles claiming in depth studies on the brain and body chemistry on both sides of the sexual argument. "I'm gay because I was born this way," or "Hey, I'm just a man who has needs." For me the question is not how I or we were born, I don't believe anyone knows enough about our brains to be able to answer just how nature and nurture, and brain and body chemistry make us who we are enough to speak definitively. The field of neuroscience itself is just beginning to make discoveries that allow us to understand only a fraction of what there is to know about our brains. While scientific studies are revealing more and more new information, many of these studies have far too many assumptions and preconceived notions that lead to foregone conclusions.

The realm of psychology is especially fluid. Trends, perspectives, and ideas change constantly. At times science has been very helpful to people, but at other times, very destructive—think lobotomy. This is why making life-altering decisions, like a lifetime of sexuality based on the current trends in psychology, is a mighty risky venture. The field has had little success studying love itself. Due to the lack of a clear definition in the scientific community, love largely goes unstudied and remains hotly debated. Thus, true love regularly gets reduced to sexual behavior only.

Since science has given us little to base the origins of our sexuality on, the question we must answer is *how were we created, according to God?* Inside each person there are all sorts of things that exist because of the world we live in. Some are good, others aren't. The only way for us to truly consider what God wants for us, is to decide what He intended long ago, in perfection. Settling for anything less would be selling ourselves, and Him, short.

So here is the question, how was Adam made? Interestingly enough this is where the Bible and Darwin agree—not that Darwin believed in Adam. The Bible says man was created by God, a thought that Darwin eventually rejected. But the Bible and Darwin do agree on one thing; there is no eternal, immortal soul within us. In fact the idea that there is one originated in pagan belief. Like in our current era, the idea permeated much of ancient culture, science, and even theories on health and medicine. When Darwin came along, and when parts of the Protestant Reformation developed both came to the same conclusion: there is no inner self that is separate from our outer self. There is only the mind and the body together that is left to make sense of the world around us and how we should relate to it. Genesis 2:7 says that God formed Adam's body, then breathed into his body the breath of life and he became a soul. Nowhere in any of scripture does it state that man was given an eternal spirit or soul. From scripture we clearly see that you cannot separate the mind and body, and there is no soul separate from our physical nature. Yet, modern psychology is teaching that what we are on the outside and what we are on the inside can be, and often are, different things.

Consider this from a well-known secular source on health, sexuality, and sexual identity:

> "Our sexuality affects who we are and how we express ourselves. There's a wide range of how people experience their sexuality. Some people are very sexual, while others experience no feelings of sexual attraction at all. Your sexuality may be influenced by your family, culture, religion, media, friends, and experiences. No matter how important sexuality is to you, we all have thoughts, desires, attractions, and values that are unique.

> "Sexuality is about much more than just sex. It includes your body, including your sexual and reproductive anatomy and body image—how you feel about your body

> - your biological sex—male, female, or intersex
>
> - your gender—being a girl, boy, woman, man, or transgender, or genderqueer
>
> - your gender identity—feelings about and how you express your gender
>
> - your sexual orientation—who you're sexually and/or romantically attracted to
>
> - your desires, thoughts, fantasies, and sexual preferences
>
> - your values, attitudes, and ideals about life, love, and sexual relationships
>
> - your sexual behaviors—including masturbation."

> "What does it mean to be a woman or man? Whether we are women or men is not determined just by our sex organs. Our gender includes a complex mix of beliefs, behaviors, and characteristics. How do you act, talk, and behave like a woman or man? Are you feminine or masculine, both, or neither? These are questions that help us get to the core of our gender and gender identity." [24]

So what this health provider is saying is that there is an inner sexuality based on feelings, thoughts, beliefs, and urges within us that may be different from our "outer self." On the outside one might be a woman,

---

24   http://www.plannedparenthood.org/health-topics/sexuality-4323.htm. 3/0.2013.

on the inside they could be a man. Some may not identify within them either gender. Along with this understanding comes the influence of socially accepted norms. They go on to present that gender and identity are largely determined by society. With this thinking, in some societies you could be more like a man, in others more like a woman, and still others like neither. It is based on a particular time and place. It's very relative. People are being taught today that who you are is based on how you feel deep within yourself. They are separating the physical nature from something else, deep within each individual. Some might call it a soul. Others might call it their inner nature. Oddly enough this defies both Darwin and the Bible.

Darwin believed that the purpose for every organism (humans included) was to pass their genes to the next generation. Gender identity confusion and even homosexuality certainly hinders the ability for a person to be able to successfully pass their desirable traits to their offspring. Arguments to somehow reconcile homosexuality and Darwinism have been made but leave adherents comparing humans to insects who have colonies with certain workers who have no offspring and how this benefits the species. These arguments are weak at best, especially considering the greater and greater incidence of homosexuality among humans today. There must be something more than natural selection at work here. Of course, Bible-believing Christians reject most of the claims of Darwin. But it serves an interesting platform to see how in this one area the Bible and Darwin agree to debunk this psycho-sexual theory.

Identity confusion and homosexuality are at even greater odds with the love of God for mankind. They leave each individual to create for themselves a system of ethics, morals, and sexuality based on an inner self and identity. It makes a person's morals in the world fluid and undetermined. It gives no credit to the sovereignty of God as creator of love and sexuality; or the peace and individuality that come only from Him. This leaves each person to determine their own destiny and happiness apart from any external creator, providential leading, lord, or judge. Said plainly this thinking makes us a god and omits a Creator and Savior in Heaven.

If sexual morality is based only on attraction, human feelings, or passions it is not based on true love (Jesus). If God is love, then love must be defined and directed by Him. All attraction and passion must be in submission to Him; otherwise, it is a different kind of love—an impostor. If identity is made up only by the perception of the mind then it allows the "soul" of a person to determine our response to rejection, abuse, pain, memories, passions, lusts, successes, failures; and upbringing to dictate who we think we are and what we will do. These expressions are common among homosexuals, and transgender people: "I just felt this way," "I felt more comfortable as a man or a woman." These should raise a red flag, especially when it comes to sexuality—a God created and holy gift. Making life-altering decisions based on feelings is a very dangerous venture. [25]

Interestingly enough, many heterosexual people have said something similar when it comes to their sex lives. "That first time felt so right," or "It felt magical," or "I feel that this is the person I am meant to be with." Our culture has us convinced that our true happiness is revealed by what we feel or that our identity *feels* free when things *feel* right. I would never try and tell a person how they feel, but how they interpret and respond to those feelings is what really matters.

However, our feelings are very fickle. They are formed from experiences, habits, insecurities, successes, etc. Feelings are attached to good memories and bad ones. So while feelings can be a good measuring stick for some things, they can also very easily lead us off the right track. Are our feelings a revelation of our identity, or do they simply reveal things about what has happened in our lives? This is why everything we feel must be translated by the word of God.

> "To the law and to the testimony! If they do not speak according to this word, it is because there is no light in them." —Isaiah 8:20

The question is not whether or not someone *feels* a certain way, the question is: are those feelings from God? Do they reveal His will and identity for us? Do my feelings reveal who I am, or do they actually reveal a greater need for a relationship with God?

Again, I am not intelligent enough to be able to say how a person is born thousands of years after creation, but what I do know is that in all of our minds there is a battle over identity. So we must ask the question: are we "sexual beings"? Did God make us this way?

Genesis tells us that God created the Earth and everything in it. He then stooped down and with His own hands created Adam from the dust of the earth. All that Adam was—the life from God and the body from the earth—was made by the hand of God Himself. There was no life in Adam that was separate from his body.

---

25   For more on this go to http://nypost.com/2013/08/06/im-a-guy-again-abc-newsman-who-switched-genders-wants-to-switch-back/

At this point there was no Eve. It was just God and Adam alone in the garden together. God intimately hand crafted Adam and breathed life into him, the only life form on Earth He did this for. Adam was Adam before his Eve came along. Adam was a man, but his manhood was not defined by a sexual relationship. In fact Adam even began his earthly duties given by God before Eve was created. His occupation was to name the animals and tend the garden.

> "Out of the ground the LORD God formed every beast of the field and every bird of the air, and brought *them* to Adam to see what he would call them. And whatever Adam called each living creature, that was its name." —Genesis 2:19 (emphasis supplied)

Did God always intend for Adam to have his Eve? Certainly. However, Adam was not *defined* by Eve or his sexual relationship with her. Did Adam's manhood and gender identity help him to understand life after Eve was created? Certainly, but Adam's sexuality came as a gift after he found His identity in God. Adam found himself established as the father of mankind by his relationship with God. In fact God took Adam through the process of naming all the animals, and finding how he fit in with this world before He created his wife. Adam's identity was not determined by his sexuality. Adam was not primarily a "sexual being." He was a child of God.

Then in Genesis 2:18 God begins the process of creating Eve. It was God who said man should not be alone, not Adam stating it living in discontent. Sex was then given to man as a gift. Marriage was given to man as a gift.

Everything in Eden was about learning, discovery, and worship. Each creation and experience in the garden was to teach them more about God. Sex is best enjoyed in this life when it is about our spouse. Ephesians five talks about a marriage being about selflessness, in fact in verses one through five, Paul is very concerned that people would misuse sex and make it about *selfishness*.

> "Therefore be imitators of God as dear children. And walk in love, as Christ also has loved us and given Himself for us, an offering and a sacrifice to God for a sweet-smelling aroma. But fornication and all uncleanness or covetousness, let it not even be named among you, as is fitting for saints; neither filthiness, nor foolish talking, nor coarse jesting, which are not fitting, but rather giving of thanks. For this you know, that no fornicator, unclean

person, nor covetous man, who is an idolater, has any inheritance in the kingdom of Christ and God." —Ephesians 5:1–5

Selflessness is the beauty of the Godhead, Father, Son, and Holy Spirit; each giving glory to one another. As Adam and Eve learned about married life, they were to learn the beauty of the Godhead as they lived to serve each other. The purpose of sex in their relationship was no different. Sex was not used to complete them as individuals, or to fulfill base desires. It was used to show them the selflessness of God. Within this selflessness they would bring forth children, another way man was to learn about the love of God. Sex was designed in the beginning to be other-centered. Today people believe that it is about discovering who a person truly is, as they have their desires fulfilled they discover their true self. This is completely opposite from what sex was created by God to be. Sex was never created to be used as a means for the focus of self-pleasure. In other words in its most pure and perfect form sex is less about how good *I* can feel, than it is about how good I can make my *spouse* feel.

Even a quick reading of Song of Solomon reveals that the two lovers are totally fixated on each other, not themselves. It is a passionate exchange where one gratifies the other through words, intimacy and sex. This same kind of selfless exchange is seen within the persons of the Godhead.

"Jesus answered, If I honor Myself, My honor is nothing. It is My Father who honors Me, of whom you say that He is your God." —John 8:54

"Jesus spoke these words, lifted up His eyes to heaven, and said: "Father, the hour has come. Glorify Your Son, that Your Son also may glorify You." —John 17:1

"And I will pray the Father, and He will give you another Helper, that He may abide with you forever— the Spirit of truth, whom the world cannot receive, because it neither sees Him nor knows Him; but you know Him, for He dwells with you and will be in you. I will not leave you orphans; I will come to you." —John 14:16-18

This selfless godliness was designed to be communicated in the relationship of human marriage and sexuality.

"… submitting to one another in the fear of God…"For this reason a man shall leave his father and mother and be joined to his wife, and the two shall become one flesh." This is a great mystery, but

I speak concerning Christ and the church. Nevertheless let each one of you in particular so love his own wife as himself, and let the wife *see* that she respects *her* husband." —Ephesians 5:21, 31–33 (emphasis supplied)

The devil wants to destroy our very identity because God has a special purpose for our identity and eventually our marriage if marriage is in His will for us. Notice this verse:

"… like a mother comforts her child, so will I comfort you over Jerusalem." —Isaiah 66:13

Please take note this is God speaking! God can act like … a woman? Haven't we always been told that God is a man? Yes, and it's probably proper to refer to Him in the male gender because that is the way Jesus referred to Him and frankly it's just grammatically correct. But please notice that the Bible refers to God as Spirit, and a Fire, among other things. What exactly is Spirit? As finite humans we can't be sure.

All of mankind was made in the image of God, not just Adam, but Adam and Eve. "Let us make *mankind* in our image, in the image of God created he *them*" (Genesis 1:26, emphasis supplied). This image was based on his physical traits in some sense, but more importantly mankind was created like Him in character. This is precisely why there is an attack today on identity and sexuality. Men were given characteristics that were to exhibit what God's character is like. In the noble and holy, self-sacrificial character of the manhood of men, God was to be seen. The same goes for women, in the noble and righteous character of women the character of God was to be seen. (see Proverbs 31)

Women are specially hand designed by God to show the world the heart and actions of God. (God help them)

Men are specially hand designed by God to show the world the heart and actions of God. (God help us)

Marriage and sex were designed by God to show the world an even fuller picture of the character of God. When you put the characteristics that God gave men and women together, the world gets to see a living, yet human example of what God is really like. Thus if Satan can confuse sexuality in the minds of people to convince them that who we are is found only through inner feelings and sexual fulfillment then we will never really be able to apply sexuality properly. Sexuality then would become a distraction (even like a false gospel) to finding who God made us to be. If you make love or sex your comfort and satisfaction, you make your lover your savior.

We were designed, like Adam, to find out who God made us to be *first* before sexuality is ever a part of our lives. Like Ecclesiastes says there is a "time for embracing and a time to abstain from embracing" (vs. 3:5). Thus through taking sex out of its proper context, Satan can confuse identities and destroy the individual characteristics God has given us as men and women to show God's character to the world. If the devil can destroy our sexuality individually, he can then destroy one of the most powerful examples God has created to show the world His glory—your marriage.

Let me give you a real life example of this. Last year I was approached by a young man who had recently been hospitalized because of severe depression. The depression was brought on by a terrible bout with stress over the lifestyle he had been living. For nearly twenty years he had been living a homosexual lifestyle. He told me that, as a child, he was repeatedly molested by his father for a period of almost ten years. During his teen years he met with a counselor who helped him talk through some of these issues, and confessed to the counselor he was very confused over his sexuality—which is quite common for abuse victims. He didn't know if he was gay, straight, or neither. The counselor worked with him for a number of months and during that time they decided together that his confusion probably meant he was really gay. So for the next fifteen years he lived a homosexual lifestyle, and had relationships with many men. Then, just a few weeks before he spoke with me, he realized he never found any peace in any of the relationships he was in. He kept thinking the next person would be the one to bring him the peace he desired. But the person never did. So he began to question his whole life. He began to feel like his life was totally out of control; that who he would have been was destroyed by his father, and possibly made even worse by his counselor. He became totally depressed. His whole life had been one confused mess. He was ashamed of himself. He was totally lost and spiraling out of control. That day he looked me in the eye and without any prompting said something that was totally profound. "All those years, all I wanted was to love and be loved. I feel like I don't know who I am." It brought tears to my eyes. He and his counselor had determined that he would be happiest by pursuing a certain sexual lifestyle, because that lifestyle was 'who he was'. In reality this sexuality destroyed him, when all he really wanted was love.

Forget an intrinsic self, or the idea of humans as sexual beings, what we are all longing for is to love and be loved. There is no human experience, or sexual identity, or marriage, or relationship with any human being that can ever make us content, and satisfied. We were made by God for a relationship with God and as we serve God we learn how to love Him like how He loved us.

> "For God so loved the world that He gave His only begotten Son, that whosoever believeth in Him should not perish, but have everlasting life. God sent His son into the word not to condemn the world, but that through Him the whole world might be saved." —John 3:16, 17

There are a number of ways that Satan loves to confuse us over what our life purpose is supposed to be. There is a heated argument over whether or not homosexuals can be 'cured'. Homosexuality is a disease every bit as much as heterosexuality can be a disease. Sexual preference is not a virus, but we certainly do need a cure. We have made sex a weakness in our very nature. We have allowed it to bring moral decay. We have told our boys that in order to be a real "man" they need to be a ladies man. We have told our girls that in order to be a real woman they need to be beautiful like Barbie; we have tried to fit them into a mold. Through the media we allow in to our homes we have let them believe the only way to be truly happy is to find their soul mate, and the best way to seek that person out is through being promiscuous. Too many children have been raised as people who crave praise rather than learning that fulfillment is about being a servant. These problems translate into sexual lifestyles, and how someone sees themselves.

What we all really need to understand is that we are children of God. Sexuality cannot be used to define us. The identity we live out should not be based on what we feel inside, or who we think we are sexually attracted to, or what our friends think, or even what modern medicine is telling us. We are not God, and we are not the Creator. Our identity should come from the One who made us. Our sexuality is only a gift. Our identity is not defined by how we fit into this world. It should be defined by how we fit into the world to come. This definition comes only from a relationship with Jesus.

A person is not to find who they are by their sexuality, they are to find who they are in God, and then enjoy the gift of sexuality, as defined by Him (if they choose to). God gave sex as a gift, not a requirement. Single people can be content and just as happy in their relationship with God as people who are married. The same goes for relationships. Our identity is not found in who we are attracted to. We find our identity in God (like Adam did) and then we find who we are to love in this world. We have it all backwards. This is why in His word God repeatedly refers to mankind's rebellion as man being unfaithful to Him.

> "Then the LORD said to me, 'Go again, love a woman *who is* loved by a lover and is committing adultery, just like the love of the LORD for the children of Israel, who look to other gods and love *the* raisin cakes *of the pagans.*'" —Hosea 3:1 (emphasis supplied)

This is why sex outside marriage is a sin. This is why sex in many marriages is unfulfilling. This is why homosexuality is sin; because mankind is seeking after love, peace, fulfillment, and identity apart from God. In the sexual gospel we are turning to our feelings and passions as a guide rather than using the perfect law of God. It is a false religion. It is running to the arms of another lover for the intimacy that God has created us to find in Him. It is running to another creator (sex, romance) to find purpose and identity. Too many people have allowed sexuality to make an identity for them because within this sexuality they feel that they will experience the most love and appreciation. Too many of us desperately create an entire identity and image for the purpose of receiving the love we so terribly desire. We crave this so madly because it is what we lost at the fall. God made man in His image. When humanity fell into sin, the image of God in man was lost. So rather than running back to God to restore His image within us, we continue to follow the lie of the serpent in the garden, "you shall be like god." It is in God that we find out who He made us to be. However we believe that satisfying earthly passions will somehow restore what we know was lost so long ago. We believe by worshipping our image we will be cured. Another false gospel.

God's Commitment to Our Sense of Self

God is committed to us to lead us, teach us about life, and help us to know the plans He has for us. He has promised to give us an identity, and we have allowed our sexual desires, insecurities, and lusts become the definition of our life. The desire of the human heart is to love others and be loved by God, and yet we keep running to other lovers to satisfy this great need in our lives. In this way we have run after a false God, the God of sex, culture, or lust, and we find no peace. We have committed adultery.

> "For I know the thoughts that I think toward you, says the LORD, thoughts of peace and not of evil, to give you a future and a hope." —Jeremiah 29:11

"Before I formed you in the womb I knew you; Before you were born I sanctified you; I ordained you a prophet to the nations."
—Jeremiah 1:5

"But let us, who are of the day, be sober, putting on the breastplate of faith and love; and for an helmet, the hope of salvation."
—1 Thessalonians 5:8

"Trust in the LORD with all thine heart; and lean not unto thine own understanding. In all thy ways acknowledge him, and he shall direct thy paths." —Proverbs 3:5, 6

"For it is God which worketh in you both to will and to do of his good pleasure." —Philippians 2:13

"And thine ears shall hear a word behind thee, saying, This is the way, walk ye in it, when ye turn to the right hand, and when ye turn to the left." —Isaiah 30:21

"Now the Lord is the Spirit; and where the Spirit of the Lord is, there is liberty. But we all, with unveiled face, beholding as in a mirror the glory of the Lord, are being transformed into the same image from glory to glory, just as by the Spirit of the Lord."
—2 Corinthians 3:17, 18

"Where were you when I laid the foundations of the earth? ... Who determined its measurements? Surely you know! Or who stretched the line upon it? To what were its foundations fastened? Or who laid its cornerstone, When the morning stars sang together, And all the sons of God shouted for joy?" —Job 38:5–7

Chapter 6
Vindication

This is where things get really exciting. Too many people separate their love lives from their spiritual lives. What if God designed them to be one? What if your sexuality and your marriage were given a special ordination by God to show salvation to the world? What if your relationship with your spouse is a human relationship that God has hand designed so that you may understand the plan of redemption and that the world may see the heart of God?

Would marriage then be just a piece of paper?

When Love Became Selfishness

Lucifer—

> "Your heart was lifted up because of your beauty; you corrupted your wisdom for the sake of your splendor." —Ezekiel 28:17

> "You have said in your heart … I will exalt my throne above the stars of God … I will be like the Most High." —Isaiah 14:13, 14

> "In the opening of the great controversy, Satan had declared that the law of God could not be obeyed, that justice was inconsistent with mercy, and that, should the law be broken, it would be impossible for the sinner to be pardoned. Every sin must meet its punishment, urged Satan; and if God should remit the punishment of sin, He would not be a God of truth and justice. When men broke the law of God, and defied His will, Satan exulted. It was proved, he declared, that the law could not be obeyed; man could not be forgiven. Because he, after his rebellion, had been banished from heaven, Satan claimed that

the human race must be forever shut out from God's favor. God could not be just, he urged, and yet show mercy to the sinner." [26]

Corrupted beauty becomes selfishness. Selfishness no longer sees beauty in service, submission and obedience. Pride becomes self-worship, yet there is no true satisfaction in self-worship. In desperation one turns to the fulfillment of lust to feel happiness. This leads to destruction.

People have the wrong idea about obedience. As long as the church has existed, people have incorrectly thought that obedience is about God granting you salvation, and blessings because you did something for Him. This actually is not obedience at all. To truly obey one must submit willingly, otherwise obeying a law becomes about self exaltation—"what I get out of the deal"—Self worship.

God has never wanted forced obedience. That's why He didn't consume Lucifer in fire long ago. He has always wanted people to obey out of love, and to submit to Him out of trust. By nature, this is something man cannot do. We are born selfish.

> "Because the carnal mind is enmity against God: for it is not subject to the law of God, nor indeed can be." —Romans 8:7

For this reason, Jesus came to this Earth to live as we live. When He was born of Mary, He was both the Son of God, and the Son of Man. This is really good news. As God, with a sinless heart, He could be our Savior. As a man who was tempted like us, yet overcame, He could be our example.

So we have to ask the question, why would Jesus do His Father's will by saving us? Is it to get something out of the deal? What more could He get? He was already God in the flesh. Therefore, why would Jesus submit to the Father and obey? The answer is simple yet profound; out of love for His Father, and out of love for us.

Jesus gave us the reason Himself:

> "Jesus said to him, 'You shall love the Lord your God with all your heart, with all your soul, and with all your mind.' This is the first and great commandment." —Matthew 22: 37, 38

Jesus said that the reason we should obey is because we love. Jesus said the same thing in John 14:15 "If you love me keep my commandments."

---

26   *The Desire of Ages.* Page 761

God doesn't want obedience because He will destroy us if we refuse. He wants us to love Him so much we submit to His loving control and let Him direct our lives. So in a very real sense full submission is complete intimacy and an expression of love.

When people think about sex and relationships, they all too soon forget about this awesome truth—God is love, so He's concerned about our love lives and our sex lives. Some of you knew this already, but perhaps this truth is even greater than you could have ever imagined.

▶ He feeds us.

▶ He gives us water to drink.

▶ He gives us a home.

▶ He gives us a loving family.

▶ He keeps us safe and defends us from enemies.

▶ He handcrafts the roses, and men are just the delivery boys.

▶ He is a strong and mighty tower.

He has been courting us our whole lives. Everything that He has brought us through is God trying to prove His worth as a worthy husband to mankind. It is simply amazing to think about it that way. God has nothing to prove, yet because He loves us enough to give us freewill, He is every second of our lives trying to earn our love.

The ultimate expression of His faithfulness to us is seen when Jesus became "one" with man. The Creator was born a man and spent His first night in an animal's feeding trough.

He became a man to be one with man.

Then again later, God forever became one with man during one terrible and beautiful weekend.

One night in a garden Jesus began to sweat great drops of blood. Why?

Here's why: 2 Corinthians 5:21 For our sake he made him to be sin who knew no sin, so that in him we might become the righteousness of God.

He traded places with us. The Father treated Him as we deserve, so that He might treat us as Christ deserves. He was separated from the One He loves so that we might be united with God forever. The Godhead became broken so that we might become whole.

One sad Friday He was hung on a cross. Here's why:

> "For the wages of sin is death, but the gift of God is eternal life in Christ Jesus our Lord." —Romans 6:23

> "And I, if I am lifted up from the earth, will draw all peoples to Myself." —John 12:32

He died the death we deserve so that we may live the life He made possible. By this act of great love He is the loving and heavenly magnet drawing your heart to His.

Friday evening—He lay dead in a tomb. Here's why:

Romans 6:3-5 Do you not know that all of us who have been baptized into Christ Jesus were baptized into his death? We were buried therefore with him by baptism into death so that, just as Christ was raised from the dead by the glory of the Father, we too might walk in newness of life. For if we have been united with him in death, we shall certainly be united with him in a resurrection.

He lived a sinless life, and surrendered it to death so that we can benefit from it. We can overcome as He overcame. We may have eternal life because God counted His death as ours and just like He was raised from death, we too will see eternity. Full surrender to the plan of salvation is needed so that He may have complete intimacy with us—that we may be "one."

Now those that love God are at *one* with Him. Remember that phrase: at one.

> "... the riches of the glory of this mystery, which is Christ in you, the hope of glory." —Colossians 1:27

Reunited

Before sin God spoke with man face to face. Through sin, Adam and Eve turned their face from Him, and didn't know how to turn back. They were made in His image, and that image was lost to sin and then we become restored to His image through Jesus.

God living within those that love Him ... The plan of redemption. ... At*one*ment ...

> "Much more then, being now justified by his blood, we shall be saved from wrath through him. For if, when we were enemies,

we were reconciled to God by the death of his Son, much more, being reconciled, we shall be saved by his life. And not only so, but we also joy in God through our Lord Jesus Christ, by whom we have now received the at*onement*." —Romans 5:9–11 (emphasis supplied)

Man *one* with God again. You've got to love a God like that! A God who would love so much that He would submit to His own penalty just so that we can live and love. The good news is that Jesus gave us the ability to love when He obeyed and died for us.

We Now May Love God and Love Each Other.

It's been Lucifer's claim that no one would love God enough to obey Him perfectly. Through His life He was tried and in His death Jesus was tortured, but His love for the Father and for us surpassed any fear, pain, or temptation. On the very night He took on our sins, His voice could be heard saying these powerful words:

"My Father, if it be possible, let this cup pass from me; nevertheless, *not as I will, but as you will*." Matthew 26:39. And in that moment, Lucifer's claims were proven untrue. Jesus submitted totally and completely and obeyed unerringly. God's will could in fact be obeyed. This obedience comes from the beauty of intimacy, selflessness, and service.

Full submission ... Complete intimacy, the very thing Lucifer believes impossible ... If there were ever a true love story, this is it. To totally trust the Father in Heaven, to love humanity so much He gave his perfect, sinless life on behalf of tiny little people on a tiny little planet—that in comparison to the rest of the Creation is smaller than a grain of sand on a beach—is true love. Everything God has designed and given man is made to focus our eyes to this matchless, powerful, love. He submitted in full obedience, surrendered to eternal death, because He is love. Is it possible that marriage, love and sex, are in fact created by God to show us the plan of redemption?

Salvation and Sex

"Human sexuality was designed by God, and was therefore, patterned after something deeply rooted in the divine identity. That something is the self-giving, other centered love that exists between the members of the Trinity. Is it any wonder, then, that human sexuality has been so deliberately malformed, perverted, and twisted into the ultimate act of anti-love self-gratification?

If sex forms a spiritual passageway of understanding into deeper intimacy with God it is not surprising that the adversary of both God and man, who stands in evil array against the atonement, would bend his powers to the task of making human sexuality a receptacle of profanity, lust, and shame." —Ty Gibson [27]

This is where things get especially incredible. There is more to the wedding vows than most people believe.

My Vows:

I Dustin, take you, Kelly to be my lawfully wedded wife. To have and to hold from this day forward: for better, for worse, for richer, for poorer, in sickness and in health, to love and cherish from this day forward until death do us part.

A man at *one* with his wife.

God's Vows:

"And not only so, but we also joy in God through our Lord Jesus Christ, by whom we have now received the *atonement*." —Romans 5:11 (emphasis supplied)

God at *one* with man.

"For this cause shall a man leave his father and mother, and shall be joined unto his wife, and they two shall be one flesh." —Ephesians 5:31

Husband and wife at *one* with each other.

Marriage is a beautiful picture of the plan of salvation.

In my wedding vows I am committing to the command given to men in Ephesians 5 "Husbands, love your wives as Christ loved the Church and gave Himself for it." In marriage I have committed to lay down my life, to set aside my personal desires and passions and be totally committed to my wife-to be 'at one' with the needs, desires, emotions, and cares of my wife, to be like Christ in submission to the Father, and in sacrifice for my wife. (God help me). This kind of intimate love that is pictured by a marriage is the same kind of intimacy that God wants with every single person. This kind of intimacy Jesus made possible through His death and resurrection.

---

27   Gibson, Ty. *A God Named Desire*. Nampa, Idaho: Pacific Press, 2010. Pg. 61.

"that they may be one as You, Father, are in Me and I in You: that they may be one in Us... just as we are one: I in them and You in Me; that they may be made perfect in one... that the love with which You loved Me may be in them, and I in them."
—John 17:21–23

As Jesus submitted to the Father and became our example through obedience to love, He is our Savior through His Godly love and life. Married people are to serve each other like Jesus served His Father in Heaven. Through this service to one another, the whole world gets to see the character of God. Through this loving submission, the whole world gets to see the plan of salvation. The whole world gets to see Jesus, and the relationship He wants with all of us. Ephesians 5 says "wives submit to your husbands," "husbands give your life for your wives," and "submit to one another in love."

Marriage and the True Character of God

Out of true love for God, Husband and wife love each other, Lucifer's claims about God, His law, and His character are proved to be a lie. This is precisely why Satan is trying to tempt us to live outside the law of God when it comes to our sexuality. This is why He is trying to destroy marriage, and sexuality all together, because he knows Godly marriages share Jesus. God gives us His commandments not to tell us that we earn His love through them, but that through submitting to Him in obedience is the only way we can be truly happy.

Godly marriages experience Jesus.

Here are some more examples of God's commitment to us:

"Behold, what manner of love the father has given unto us that we may be called the sons and daughters of God." —1 John 3:1

"I will never leave you nor forsake you." —Hebrews 13:5

"For I will restore health to you, and your wounds I will heal, declares the LORD." —Jeremiah 30:17

"And I will betroth you to me forever. I will betroth you to me in righteousness and in justice, in steadfast love and in mercy. I will betroth you to me in faithfulness. And you shall know the LORD. "And in that day I will answer, declares the LORD. ... I will answer the heavens... and they shall answer the earth, and the earth shall answer the grain, the wine, and the oil ... and I will sow her for myself in the land. And I will have mercy on No Mercy, and I will say to Not My People, 'You are my people'; and he shall say, 'You are my God.'" —Hosea 2:19–21

The reason God cares about our love lives, our sexuality, and our marriage is because He has hand designed the union of man and wife to show the world what he is really like. In fact the word "know" comes up frequently in the Old Testament when referring to God's desire for a relationship with people. This root word from the Hebrew is often the same word used when Adam and Eve "knew" (Genesis 4:1) each other and conceived a son. You see sexuality itself is a physical, spiritual, and emotional picture God gave to man to know both how intimately the persons (Father, Son, Holy Spirit) of the Godhead love each other, and in kind the relationship that God wants with us.

In Jesus and the Gospel self ends and love is realized.

Godly Desire

God desired unity with us so much, that He gave everything so that we might be saved. God really desires to be one with man—just like He made us in the beginning. God gave sex to man so that we may understand the intimacy that He desires with all of us. Sex was created so that we may know that in true intimacy "self" ends and "us" is fully realized. The only way that sinful man can experience this is through submitting to the selfless nature of God. As God dwells in us we learn to set selfishness aside, then the sexual and intimate relationship between a husband and a wife will thrive. Not that God is a sexual being, but one of the clearest ways God shows us what His character is really like is through the loving, and powerful sexual "oneness" between a husband and wife.

A New Definition of Purity

If sex is merely for personal pleasure why then do so many people feel empty and unfulfilled after sex? Wouldn't they after feeling personal pleasure be totally satisfied? Sex was made for a specific reason, for a specific context. As Jesus showed His love for the Father by submitting to His will, Jesus bonded Himself to humanity for eternity. As a husband and a wife commit to each other for life, sex becomes the ultimate experience through the fulfillment of the other spouse.

Satan has made the world believe a lie about what love is, and thus made us believe a lie about who God is. But the Holy Spirit wants to use your marriage to vindicate His Holy and loving name.

"And I will vindicate the holiness of my great name. ... And the nations will know that I am the LORD, declares the LORD God, when through you I vindicate my holiness before their eyes."
—Ezekiel 36:23

Most people think it's their life's mission to find true love. What they don't realize is that we are not to find true love. True love found us in the plan of salvation through Jesus Christ. "While we were yet sinners Christ died for us" (Romans 5:8). We are not to find true love, however, we are to show true love. We show true love in our loving submission to the commandments of God, and our unity with Him. We show true love through obeying the Holy Spirit teaching us how to love our husbands and wives. God cares about your love life. By making your love life *His* definition of incredible, you experience Him and get to show the whole world what He is really like. As a husband and wife are one in their sexual relationship, in purpose, in selflessness, in mission, the world sees the plan of salvation and the character of God.

Three C(h)ords

"Follow your heart" they say—but I know that if I do
I'd be following something I can't know—deceitful and untrue
I couldn't love you if I tried, I couldn't find a way
Unless my heart is led by God, I'll only go astray

If we want to be one heart, one flesh, one instead of two
There's got to be three cords woven—God and me and you
If our hearts burn within us with a fire that consumes
Only then can we say I love you

God is love. He gives to us a priceless gift that's free
He gave Himself, He gave His all, unconditionally
I want to love you like He does—Lord give me eyes to see
The only way I can is if you live inside of me

If we want to be one heart, one flesh, one instead of two
There's got to be three cords woven—God and me and you
If our hearts burn within us with a fire that consumes
Only then can we say I love you

Love is kind, love never fails it ain't boastful, proud or rude
It bears all things, believes all things, rejoices in the truth
Love will never seek her own, love's patient, love endures
If we want a love like that here's what we'll have to do

If we want to be one heart, one flesh, one instead of two
There's got to be three cords woven—God and me and you
If our hearts burn within us with a fire that consumes
Only then can we say I love you

The love of God is the only love—the only one that's true
The love of God is the only one that's true

It's the love that binds us, it binds us tightly—stronger than the grave
What God has joined together now, let no one separate
This love is for forever—it's for eternity
Cos' the wellspring of our love is the One who is and was and will be

If we want to be one heart, one flesh, one instead of two
There's got to be three cords woven—God and me and you
If our hearts burn within us with a fire that consumes
Only then can we say I love you
And I love you with a love that's true

—Josh Cunningham, From the album *Into Tomorrow*

Chapter 7
Salvation by Soul Mates

I t's question and answer time at my seminars and her hand is always the first one to shoot into the air. As it does, all her friends roll their eyes because they know what is coming. They have spent countless hours in her dorm room or on the phone consoling her after many failed relationships. "Why can't I find my soul mate?" "Why doesn't someone really love me?" "Why do guys have to be so awful?" You know the drill.

So her hand flies up and she asks me something like "Why can't I find true love?" Perhaps you are laughing at yourself a little right now because you may have felt much the same way at some point. My answers to this question have changed over the years, but recently I have come to the knowledge that the whole mess we get ourselves into over love ... is Plato's fault.

Yes, Plato from classical Greece— Socrates' pupil. How could it be his fault, you ask? Let me expand your mind. Plato wrote a very famous book called the *Symposium*, a collection of arguments about what love is. In this work, one of the 'actors' or philosophers discussing the love question presents a widely held religious belief of the Greeks at that time.

Greek mythology taught that at Creation mankind was made with two heads; some had a male and female head, some two males, others with two female. Zeus, a Greek god became angry with man and chopped all humans in half— including their soul. So man has been destined ever since to walk the earth in search of their *SOUL MATE* or *OTHER HALF*. Plato wrote that only through knowledge, trial and error can a person find their soul mate to achieve platonic love and true peace. The Greeks also believed this explained homosexuality. Some people had a same-sex soul mate because they were created with two same-sex heads.

This ideology filtered into the Greek arts, was passed down through time and resurfaced during the Enlightenment. Is it possible so many people make a disaster of their love lives because they believe what the Greeks thought and not what God says? What part of this mythology is still around today?

1. Love is found, not made. If we are all in a desperate pursuit to find our soul mate, then allowing God to work on our character is far less important than the search for our "other half." This is a major reason that the average number of sexual partners for men is 15 and for women is 8[28] and why we have a date around, sleep around culture. We believe that the best way to find our soul mate is to date as many people as possible to give ourselves the best chance. It's like buying thousands of lottery tickets. People even believe that to make sure you are a sexual match you must try each other out sexually before marriage. Interestingly enough seeking 'soul mate' love becomes decidedly self-centered. It's about someone fitting "me" not "me" growing to become a good fit for "someone."

God created Eve, not out of Adam's discontent, but to be Adam's equal. Eve was made from his rib because a rib protects our vital organs—including our heart. Eve was a wonderful gift for Adam to share his life with. Adam was a gift for Eve to share her life with. If you believe that Eve was created because Adam wasn't happy you seriously have degraded women. You may have even made her like a prostitute.

Symposium teaches that half of a person plus half of a person makes one whole person. God teaches that one person (with Him) plus one person (with Him) makes one person. In fact, it is the merging of two people that makes for the "one flesh" relationship. It is a powerful moment when we realize that the relationship built on love and "oneness" within the godhead was severed on the cross. Jesus cried out, "My God, My God why have you forsaken me?" (Matthew 27:46). He felt totally cut off and like an enemy of the Father for us. The Godhead severed its relationship so that we might be made whole. To contrast this truth with Greek Mythology it was the selfishness of Zeus that caused him to cut humanity in half, leaving them to desperately search for their soul mate. In scripture it was the Godhead that was severed so that man could be made whole. If this is true we are never incomplete when we have Jesus. We believe a lie when we believe that we can ever be made complete by falling in love, or that somehow we are lost without being in love. An 80's love song went like

---

28   Anjani, Chandra Et al. "Sexual Behavior, Sexual Attraction, and Sexual Identity in the United States: Data From the 2006–2008 National Survey of Family Growth." *National Health Statistics Reports*. 36.March 2011 n. page. Web. 17 Oct. 2013. <http://www.cdc.gov/nchs/data/nhsr/nhsr036.pdf>.

this, "I can't live, if livin' is without you." This couldn't be farther from the truth. We can live because God was broken. We are whole because He was cut off.

God Writes Love Stories

Nearly every marriage story from the Bible is an arranged marriage. Does God pick ONE person for us to be with? No, that's not free will. But He fashions certain people to be a better match with us than others. To be a compliment for someone else we must allow Him to change us into becoming all of the qualities of love mentioned in 1 Corinthians 13. Most of us think that 1 Corinthians 13 is something we "find" with someone else. Arranged marriages worked in Bible times because they did not expect all of love to be found before marriage. They realized that they had to grow together. In fact, recent studies done in eastern cultures which still practice arranged marriages revealed that couples that have been married for many years report that love is the reason that their marriage survived. Great marriages are centered on God and our spouse, not the opposite.

2. The harder it is, the more "true" love it must be. Pagan thinking made its way into such outlets as Greek tragedies, Shakespeare, *Aladdin* and *The Notebook.* We believe that the more forbidden, the more difficult, the more trying, the truer the love story—we just didn't know it was Zeus who was making it so difficult. Did you know that for over 1000 years love sickness was diagnosed by doctors as a mental disorder? Just think of it, when people fall "in love" they display symptoms of eating disorders, Obsessive Compulsive Disorder, insomnia, sociopathic tendencies, and psychopathic behavior! It was first diagnosed in ancient Greece by Hippocrates as we have said in an earlier chapter. It seems that the Greek way of thinking about love leads people to do crazy things for love. This explains a ton in our own culture.

Love at first sight, (often cured by a second look) is an interesting thing. Often people see a person they are attracted to and automatically apply to them every quality they value in a potential spouse; without ever having spoken to them. They will then fight for their "soul mate" to the death and regardless of the consequences, only to find later that the person they fell in love with was not the person they thought them to be. Other marriages are based on the idea that someone with rough edges will change "for me." Interestingly enough, it is those rough edges that must change before love can actually work. No marriage is easy, but tragedy and hardship are not a sign that love is "written in the stars." In fact those negative character traits are the very thing God Himself must remove before we can ever be a fit candidate for marriage. If someone is truly a great compliment for our lives, marriage should be a smooth transition, not a *Romeo and Juliet*-like tragedy! Again to disagree with the pagan Greeks, to have a great marriage we must be content (Philippians 4:11–13) first. No person has ever been designed to make us complete and content. If you are expecting a human being to make you feel whole, loved, and accepted, you will be waiting your whole life. If you look to God to make you totally happy and be the source of your heart's desires, you, in actuality, will enroll in the best training school possible to be a great mate.

Soul Mates and Bible Prophecy

Because of the great deception about love and God's character, the Three Angel's Messages in Revelation 14:6–12 are crucially important. The first angel in verse six reminds us of who God is (Creator, Judge, Savior), the second angel reminds the world what God is like (Babylon is a symbol for false religion based on a false picture of God), and the third angel shouts to the world about how God alone saves (Salvation either comes through selfish means, or through Jesus alone). So, if God is love, we can replace His name in this passage with "Love," and reveal the devil's plans by saying the opposite of the Three Angels' Messages. If the devil can make you believe a lie about:

1. What Love is, then he can make you believe a lie about

2. What love does, and he can make you believe a lie about

3. How Love saves.

It seems simple but it is diabolical and it has destroyed millions. So the question stands for us today, what saves us? Finding our soul mate like Plato would tell us? Or does the true love of Jesus Christ, really save us? If so, stop starving in the desert in pursuit of romance and acceptance. Come to the Bread of Life, the Water from the Well that will never run dry, the Lamb of God, the One who sings over us with gladness, the Beginning and the End, the one who breathes out the stars and counts the number of hairs on our heads; Jesus Christ.

So who will it be, your 'soul mate' or Jesus?

Chapter 8
Marriage and the "Equally Yoked" Question

he question box fills up at every one of my seminars. The questions are always diverse and interesting. Many of them I can answer, others I can't. Every Q&A session brings new questions, some of them troubling, like the questions about children as young as five and six affected by pornography. Other questions are funny, like the time a young man asked me how to snag a "hot" wife. But at every session I get more than one question about dating, and ultimately marrying someone who is not in the church. Many of these questions come from people who are already in a relationship with someone of a different faith, or no faith at all. Others are just worried that they will never meet someone of the same faith and want to explore other options. For many single people, it seems much easier to find someone outside the church than it is to find someone in it.

This method seems perfectly reasonable. "Outsiders" are attractive, nice, some of them Christ-loving people, yet deep inside we know they aren't exactly who God wants for us. Why? Why do we have that nagging suspicion that God desires us to marry people who are of the same faith? Is it just because that's what we've always heard? Is it because we think it's what our church expects? Or is there something much deeper and more powerful at work? Is there really something intended for marriage that gives it power, making it vital that we look at the world with the same set of faithful eyes and hearts as our spouse? The following will be a few things you may not have thought about as to why it's so important to allow God to lead you to the right person in the church at the right time.

1. It's About Knowing You.

We all know that God is trying to transform us and make us into what He is—real unselfish love. The whole Christian life is about God using His power to transform us into His image because we can't do that by ourselves. So Satan (God's enemy) has tried to take romance (something beautiful) and mingle it with selfishness. Therefore there is a battle over our minds and our hearts. Will we become more selfish, or will we become more like God? For those of us who are Christians we can tell God is doing something in our lives, we see Him taking over and that is a really great thing. In an inexplicable way it makes us feel more like ourselves when we become more like Him (we were made in His Image). Therefore it is Jesus Himself who makes us who we are. It is God who helps us use the gifts He has given us. In Him we find true contentment and satisfaction. So this creates a question: if Jesus makes us who we are, how can someone really know us if they don't know Jesus? Can you imagine how frustrating and limiting a marriage would be where you don't feel fully known by your spouse? Perhaps some of you reading this can relate to this very dilemma. Many young adults simply do not see the theological and practical conflict that occurs when they try to open up their heart about what God is doing and the other person just simply cannot comprehend any of it. It is absolutely vital that both spouses are looking at God with similar eyes, and the world with a similar worldview. Each Christian denomination has its own way of looking at Jesus. Their individual perspectives affect what each one believes about God's character. If one desires to be changed into His character it is important that husband and wife see God through the same "God-view." Interestingly enough, most of us would put "same faith" at the top of our list of qualities of a future spouse. Every person dating or married to someone outside the church hopes their beloved will convert one day. Perhaps deep down we know something major is missing when faith does not agree, yet quite often other priorities get in the way. If we really want to be known by our husband or wife, they must know the One who makes us who we are. No question.

Life Happens

The other side to this is obvious. There are logistical issues. How will the kids be raised? How will you use time and money? I have done pre-marital counseling (but never married them) with couples in the past that before the wedding disagreed about these issues, and when life starts happening they end up with serious conflict. What day will you go to church? What if sports or other activities interfere with church hours? What about tithes and offerings? These issues are difficult enough in marriages that do share common beliefs about God. How much harder is it in homes where people do not agree about their faith?

2. It's About Knowing God.

As we have already studied in Ephesians 5 the Bible tells us that husbands should love and serve their wives like Jesus loved and served the church. Again, this is about becoming like Jesus. The woman a man marries should make them want to love like Christ, and serve like Christ. Ephesians 5 also instructs women to respectfully support their husband and help him grow into the person God has made him to be. It says that this work at times may require that women lay aside some of their own plans so that men can experience the needed growth. Either way you look at it, it's about becoming like Jesus—serving, and loving selflessly for the good of the ones we love. This love, this kind of marriage, was designed to show husband and wife the character of God. As the wife loves and serves the husband, he sees Jesus. As the husband loves and serves the wife, she sees Jesus. Within their service to one another their hearts are being led by God Himself. They are participating in the actions of Christ. If marriage is about being changed into God's character, this desire and this knowledge should be central in the minds of both husband and wife. If you can't agree on wanting this transformation into God's character, it can make for a very frustrating and incomplete life. God himself is a relationship between persons: Father, Son and Holy Spirit. The three persons in the One Being of God all share the same purpose, vision, and way of thinking. A marriage where this like-minded existence prevails makes for a powerful union that teaches us about God Himself; how He loves, how He works, how He thinks.

Decisions, Decisions

Please let me ask you a few questions. If marriage is really all about knowing and showing what God is really like, how important is our decision about who we marry? It is important that people who are thinking about marriage do some prayerful self-evaluation. Do they find themselves interested in people whom the true Jesus already lives in, or people who He is trying to introduce Himself to? How they answer this question will reveal how ready they are to start thinking about marriage, and how vulnerable they are to believing a lie about what true love is. Letting God write your love story makes for a much better life. God has amazing plans for your marriage. Single people should start praying for their future spouse now, even if they don't know who that will be. Growing to know Jesus more today is the single best practice for marriage preparation; to become someone's ideal help at the right time. Their decisions today will affect how powerfully Jesus may shine through their marriage tomorrow.

I hope you look at marriage in a whole new way. There might still be a conflict in your heart because you doubt how you will ever find someone like what we have described above. But have no fear. God is in the business of writing love stories. When we ask Him to help us see as He sees, and love as He loves, the transformation that takes place within us will lead us to an incredible marriage.

For further study please read: Genesis 2:22–24; Mark 10:6–9; Proverbs 5:8–18, 12:4, 19:4, 30:18–19, 31, 1 Corinthians 11:1, 2; 1 John 2:3-4; Ephesians 5, 6; _The Adventist Home_ Chapters 3, 5, 6, 7

Chapter 9

Pornography and the Destruction of Sex

She came to me a very nervous woman. She had been sitting in the back of the auditorium as I was preaching to a group of college students. She had heard me give a presentation on pornography and its effects on the brain and life. Once all the students had cleared out, this middle-aged woman walked up to me and with a nervous voice said, "I think I have a problem." These kinds of greetings don't surprise me anymore. I have seen the power of the Holy Spirit work in so many amazing ways, people desperately want to be delivered from the grip of sexual sins, so they just open up.

She went on to tell me that for the last five years she had been watching more and more pornographic videos on the internet. She told me at first it was mainly out of curiosity, and then it became something else. For many years she had struggled with depression, and she quickly began to realize that when she watched pornography, she seemed to feel better for the brief time she would see it. She told me that she began to watch it less out of sexual desire, and more out of the desire to feel "alive." As she was talking to me, my mind went immediately to a friend of mine in high school who used to be heavy into drugs. He had said the exact same thing, that when he used, it would make him feel "alive." I went through the basic steps to recovery from addiction with her that I will share later in this chapter, had prayer with her and gave a referral to a local Christian counselor. As I left, my mind was deep in thought. It had never occurred to me before that people would use pornography to self-medicate. The following week I was presenting to another college group and a young man who was a leader of one of the collegiate groups came to talk with me and said nearly the exact same thing. He was stressed, feeling down and some porn minimized on his roommate's computer screen caught his eye. He watched it and immediately felt something that made him feel better and relaxed.

I am often asked to address issues like pornography use and masturbation. The latter topic seems to be particularly perplexing for many Christian writers. Often, the answers as to why people shouldn't masturbate are very shallow and don't seem well thought out. Many times, they boil it down to "it's a sin," and often leave it at that. The reasons to abstain from masturbation, however, are far more complex, and tied closely in with the reasons why porn is so self-destructive.

Pornography is nothing new in the human experience. There are cave drawings thousands of years old in various parts of the world that depict sexually explicit behavior. It seems that as long as sex has existed, there have been pictures about sex.

Covenant Eyes, a ministry dedicated to helping with the porn epidemic, compiled a wonderful e-book titled, *The Porn Free Church*[29]. In this book they list seven reasons people use pornography:

1. **Physical Lust**—Playing on a person's natural desire for sex, Satan has created for us a worship problem. Rather than worshipping God we become fixated on images of created things, "...traded the glory of the immortal God for images resembling mortal man and birds and animals and creeping things" (Rom. 1:23). Pornographers are basically modern day idol makers. The sculptors no longer work wood, or chisel stone, but utilize cameras, lighting and makeup. With these false gods, we commit the sins of lust (Ezek 14:3).

2. **Passive Pleasure**—this is a great temptation to men especially because they get to experience the benefits of sexual pleasure without the God created work of emotional intimacy. As a model looks pleasingly at you from a picture or a video, all the feelings and chemicals of attraction are there, but there is no genuine human being to bond with and work to win over. There is no virtue to add to the pleasure. This begins a dangerous hardening of the heart characteristic of people who use porn as passive pleasure. It's an especially damaging temptation because it destroys the very nature of sex designed by God.

3. **Escape**—Because sex triggers a physical release and stress reduction, people start feeling they "deserve" the release and the "special treat" their brains experience through a quick rush of mental and physical self-stimulation; like taking a vacation. Ironically

---

29   Altrogge, Stephen et al. *The Porn Free Church*. Covenant Eyes. 2013. eBook.

this is the same reason a binge drinker gives to go out on a Friday night and get wasted.

4. **Secrecy**—Internet porn is one of the easiest ways to have an affair without anyone finding out. It's easy to hide, and is easily accessible. Yet, to use the old Latin phrase "Coram Deo"—before the face of God there are no secrets. We must realize there is nothing we can hide from Him. Coupled with some of the other deceiving reasons people use porn, the perceived secrecy is very attractive.

5. **Pride**—To quote Covenant Eyes, "For many guys, lust is not the only thing driving their fixation on pornography, masturbation, and fantasy. It's also motivated by pride or self-worship" (p. 34). When a person has a crush on the latest actor or actress, a photo of a provocative, sexually insinuating look from that celebrity can be easily translated to be that celebrity's sexual desire for the person viewing the picture. In reality this kind of pleasure is actually self-worship because the celebrity is only pretending to worship the spectator. The person in the movie or picture becomes a vessel for their self-worship. Sin in fact happens first in the mind, and this self-pleasure is the fruit of a type of self-worship.

6. **False Intimacy**—Any time a person is feeling alone, all a person has to do is flip on their laptop and there is the object that makes them feel pleasure. It is an intimacy that is manufactured and the person becomes dependent on the fake "love" created in their mind. The person watching the porn has to do nothing to maintain a relationship with a real human being, only to turn on the computer or open the magazine. Ironically this is happening in the world of social media as well. People are becoming more and more dependent on how many followers they can achieve on Twitter, and how many "likes" their posts can get on Facebook. It doesn't matter who is reading the posts as long as someone responds. In reality it's not a person we are getting satisfaction from it's actually just a machine. Like never before people are connecting more and more with inanimate objects.

7. **The Forbidden**—"Stolen water is sweet, and bread eaten in secret is pleasant" (Proverbs 9:17 ESV). Sin has an allure, it plays on our pleasure centers in our brain, the selfishness of our hearts, and the propensities to sin that are ingrained in our nature. People in

our society are becoming increasingly "turned on" by the taboo, or things that seem sinful.

Let me add two more reasons that people have shared with me to explain why they use porn.

1. **Control**—More and more today, people are feeling like their lives are out of control. Using porn, and ultimately masturbation, they feel like in that moment they can control their feelings, their pleasure, and their lives. Our society expects people to be in control and ignores the fact that God is ultimately directing our lives. Using brain chemistry and sexual pleasure people feel that they can retake the reins.

2. **To supplement their marital sex lives**—in many marriages one spouse simply has more of a sex drive than the other. Since they feel that they have a greater need than their spouse they feel justified to satisfy this need with porn. What many of these people realize later is that porn does not actually satisfy the need, but instead makes sex with their spouse increasingly more dissatisfying.

Given these very solid and real life reasons, what is it that makes porn and masturbation such a temptation? What is going on? The Bible says this:

> "For the creation was subjected to futility, not willingly, but because of him who subjected it, in hope that the creation itself will be set free from its bondage to corruption and obtain the freedom of the glory of the children of God. For we know that the whole creation has been groaning together in the pains of childbirth until now. And not only the creation, but we ourselves, who have the first fruits of the Spirit, groan inwardly as we wait eagerly for adoption as sons, the redemption of our bodies." —Romans 8:20–23 (ESV)

The scripture says that all of creation, especially our bodies are longing to be restored to the perfection that once was. We are all trying desperately to get back to Eden.

> "Adam was crowned king in Eden. To him was given dominion over every living thing that God had created. The Lord blessed Adam and Eve with intelligence such as He had not given to any other creature. He made Adam the rightful sovereign over all the works of His hands. Man, made in the divine image, could contemplate and appreciate the glorious works of God in nature." [30]

---

30   White, Ellen. *The Story of Redemption*. Hagerstown, MD: EG White Estate, 2010. 7. Print.

In the perfect Creation there was no such thing as depression, pain, stress, loneliness, and heartache. Originally, the mind was full and complete. The chemicals and workings of the brain were perfect and whole. The publication *The Scientific American* reported in an interesting article about the power of our minds,, "the brain represents three percent of the body's weight and uses 20 percent of the body's energy.[31]"

Our brains are powerful and amazing machines hand crafted by God. In its original state, the intellect and happiness of Adam would have been astounding to behold. Deep within we all long for that complete mind to be restored because we struggle with daily life and the "happy chemicals" never linger long enough. The neurons that give us vitality and vigor don't fire enough, and the chemicals that make us feel content aren't around indefinitely. Bible-believing Christians know we are working with a seriously downgraded mind. One way that people try to make up for the deficiencies in the mind is with medication. Mental health professionals diagnose them for depression, anxiety, and other mental disorders. One very dangerous thing others do is self-medicate. They use illegal drugs, undiagnosed prescription drugs, and a number of other things to deal with pain and mental struggles. What every person wishes is that their mind could be restored to the perfection of the world when there was no depression, anxiety, eating disorders, discontentment, obsession, etc. During sexual activity and porn use the brain releases a cocktail of chemicals that we all wish would last indefinitely. Here is a list:

Dopamine: During sexual arousal increased dopamine in the brain produces extremely focused attention. This chemical causes each spouse to focus intensely on the other at the exclusion of everything else around them; each spouse feels that the other is a direct extension of the other. Sadly because of this chemical people connect in the same way with pornography on their TV or computer screen. While this chemical can create an intense satisfaction in connection between husband and wife, it is also associated with craving and dependency in addiction. It has such an intense effect on the brain, we tend to want more and more of whatever stimulus created its release.

Norepinephrine: This chemical generates exhilaration and increased energy by giving the body a boost of natural adrenaline.

---

31   Boyd, Robynn. "Do People Really Only Use 10% of Their Brains." *Scientific American.* Scientific American, 07 02 2008. Web. 3 Oct. 2013. http://www.scientificamerican.com/article. cfm?id=people-only-use-10-percent-of-brain

Norepinephrine has also been linked to raising memory capacity. This is why sexual experiences are so easily retrieved in the memory. Norepinephrine actually 'etches' images and memories in our minds.

Testosterone: _This is known as the hormone of sexual desire in both men and women. For men however, it is the key hormone of desire, triggering feelings of positive energy and well-being._

Oxytocin: _This relaxes and puts a person at ease, it lowers blood pressure, it blunts sensitivity to pain and stress, and eventually induces sleep. Oxytocin is also the chemical of bonding, creating moments of happiness and close intimacy with a person or porn, making another gateway for addiction._

Serotonin: _This natural chemical is released bringing on a deep feeling of calmness, satisfaction and release from stress. Anti-depressant drugs like Prozac are designed to increase levels of serotonin. Serotonin has been labeled for many years in science as the happiness chemical._

Everyone an Addict

You see, we are all drug users, desperately trying to manufacture the kinds of chemicals that will make us feel safe, bonded, secure, content, focused, calm, loved and happy. God created our minds to function in top condition, this was the experience of mankind when created, and this is what we are all longing for. Since we are all longing for our minds to work as they were designed, some people try to manufacture it through overeating, addictions, others through porn, still others through promiscuity. We all struggle with something, yet every attempt to get back to Eden that is not centered on and created by Jesus is a futile and sinful act. Whenever we rely on ourselves for restoration we will end up in destruction. Essentially, this is what most porn users become addicted to—the mental cocktail that for a fleeting moment tells their brains and bodies that everything is OK.

> "If you diligently heed the voice of the LORD your God and do what is right in His sight, give ear to His commandments and keep all His statutes, I will put none of the diseases on you which I have brought on the Egyptians. For I am the LORD who heals you." —Exodus 15:26

Many of us try, through sexuality, to heal our hurting, or stressed minds. Outside of marriage this attempt will bring heartache and destruction. Inside of marriage this is too much pressure on our spouse, for they were never created to be our healer. Sin truly does begin in the mind (Matthew 5:28). God sees our outward behavior as a reaction of our fallen nature and a condition of our own helplessness. Giving in to lust brings some people pleasure, and through that pleasure they are trying to satisfy a much deeper need that can only be filled by God. Others know their helplessness and enflame their lust in an attempt to control a life that is spinning out of control.

Porn use and masturbation will create in the human mind a bonding to a computer screen, or a mental image. It will decrease sexual satisfaction with your current or future spouse. It makes bonding with real spouses and even platonic relationships with friends increasingly more strained and difficult. It becomes addicting because people become dependent on this form of drug to take their mind to a false Eden. For many, porn use and masturbation become increasingly more frequent and deviant. It will create addiction and baggage that can last a lifetime. Like a drug, the dependency creates a tolerance where greater and more powerful doses are needed to achieve the original high. There are many people who spend hours every day watching pornography. They often miss work and forsake human contact because of it.

The Effects of Porn in Real Life

If you are still unconvinced by the problem with porn let me tell you another true story. After one of my presentations, a father approached me and told me that he had been a long time porn user. He had a private office in his home where he would watch his videos on the computer and when he would leave the room he would minimize the videos on the screen to watch another time. One day, he came in to his office and found a video he had minimized back up on the screen. He forgot about it until one day it happened again. He started looking for his ten-year-old son who he found in his seven-year-old daughter's room. What he saw shocked and broke him. He found his son practicing some of the things he had seen on his computer on his younger sister. At that moment, this father knew he had a problem and looked for help. The disgusting and sinful world of porn had infiltrated his own home, not just his mind. It was no longer private and personal, now it had affected his family for a lifetime. My friends, please do not take porn use lightly, it is a serious and dangerous tool of Satan himself. Another false gospel he uses to trick our minds to feel like we are back in the perfection of Eden, while we are actually headed down a road that will consume us and our family. One of the most troubling things about pornography is that it's fake. The scenes are staged and the actors are playing parts that they themselves are often ashamed of. The actors sustain injuries and even contract sexually transmitted diseases. The allure of porn is that it tricks your mind into thinking you're an active part of the pleasure that is taking place before your eyes when in reality, the people engaged in the behavior themselves are not even enjoying it.

Going to Rehab

Porn use does affect more than just the user; it affects our relationships with nearly everyone in our lives. So, who needs help to overcome? The answer is—everyone. Jesus said that sin begins in the mind and heart (Matthew 5:27–28). The weaknesses we have and the struggles we endure make us insanely vulnerable to lusting after pleasure because we think it will save us from the struggles of this world. This battle manifests itself in different people in different ways. For some its jealousy and pride, others lust, others addiction, etc. We all must realize that there is a way of escape for all of us. Jesus wants to renew our minds and hearts.

> "I beseech you therefore, brethren, by the mercies of God, that you present your bodies a living sacrifice, holy, acceptable to God, *which is* your reasonable service. And do not be conformed to this world, but be transformed by the renewing of your mind, that you may prove what *is* that good and acceptable and perfect will of God." —Romans 12:1, 2

In this verse God makes a promise, and we can hold him to it. The place we all need healing is in our hearts, we can battle and struggle all we want with a sinful behavior and deal with the outward act, but if our hearts are not changed, nothing has changed for us at all. You can overcome a sinful act or habit, but if you don't change a sin-dependent heart, that sin will creep up somewhere else in life. As we surrender to Him we also need to help each other gain the victories in the areas where they are frail.

We must demand from ourselves trustworthiness.

A common theme that I keep hearing from young adults is that they don't trust their church to help them with their struggles. We must be able to trust each other. For far too long we have been benefitting from the sins of others by making ourselves feel better for judging someone else. It is far easier to deal with someone else's sins than it is to deal with our own. We are called to be the body of Christ. A true body suffers when any one of its parts ache. When there is a virus or an injury the body immediately sends the needed body chemistry and energy to the place where the pain exists. We need to start acting like "the body," otherwise, we are going to self-destruct.

Even people who never watch porn still use sins in their lives to try and manufacture peace, love and reduce stress. This is why the body of believers called the church has been instructed to help each other stand and overcome. The places where I am weak, my friends are strong. Where they are weak, I am strong. The element we are most direly missing is trustworthiness to feel comfortable asking each other for help.

> "Brethren, if a man is overtaken in any trespass, you who are spiritual restore such a one in a spirit of gentleness, considering yourself lest you also be tempted. Bear one another's burdens, and so fulfill the law of Christ. For if anyone thinks himself to be something, when he is nothing, he deceives himself. But let each one examine his own work, and then he will have rejoicing in himself alone, and not in another. For each one shall bear his own load." —Galatians 6:1–5

If we are going to solve the sin problem, we have to help each other through our addictions. We need to hold each other accountable with love and genuine concern. Below you will see why being reliant on each other is so vitally important.

Here are four of the most important practical steps that could literally save your life. This is the most practical, easy and successful method for porn addiction recovery I have learned:

Elephant in the Room

Do you watch porn? Do you go to a website specifically because you might see something sexual? When you are stressed, or bored, is porn the first thing that you think about? Does porn jump into your mind when you are intimate with your wife or husband? Does it interfere with your daily life, money, or time? Do you daydream about something or someone depicted in the videos, or pictures? Are you drawn to websites or magazines that you know will bring sexual arousal? Do you feel depressed or anxious and use it as a release? Do you know that adult films and rated "R" movies are inappropriate and still find yourself watching them?

If you can answer yes to any of these questions there is good news! You can apply these four easy steps to overcome. The great news about these steps is that they can also be used to avoid the problem all together.

1. **Honesty**—Porn use is sin; a very alluring, attractive sin, but it's still sin. You have to be honest with yourself. Denial will never bring victory. You have to realize that in yourself you have no power to overcome, and you need help.

    "If we confess our sins, he is faithful and just to forgive us our sins and to cleanse us from all unrighteousness." —1 John 1:9

Being honest with yourself and God is the very first step. Honesty doesn't stop with God. If you need to talk to your spouse or someone else that has been affected by your porn use, it is absolutely necessary at this sensitive beginning. Asking for forgiveness from people we may have hurt is so important. You also may need their support for the steps ahead. If you are married and need to confess to your spouse, understand that they may feel betrayed. It takes time to regain the trust you lost. Counseling is often needed in these circumstances because it may take a third party to help sort through some of the feelings of betrayal. A porn user usually feels that they have not betrayed trust because they have never engaged with a real human being. This, however, is part of the issue we already discussed. Porn makes the user believe that they are in nearly complete fidelity, while emotionally crushing the spouse of the user. Spouses of the porn user will often feel betrayed, humiliated, inadequate, used, and embarrassed. Rebuilding trust and intimacy takes time, direct effort, and often intervention that involves forgiveness and a slow process of rebuilding.

2. **Help**—more education is pivotal. Jesus promises that:

    "If you love Me, keep My commandments. And I will pray the Father, and He will give you another Helper, that He may abide with you forever—the Spirit of truth, whom the world cannot receive, because it neither sees Him nor knows Him; but you know Him, for He dwells with you and will be in you." —John 14:15–17

God promises to be with us and teach us the path to overcome sin. But, through providence and godly relationships, he also promises to lead us to people and resources that can help us. There are also many people who have mental health struggles; perhaps a past filled with abuses that need professional counseling. This help is absolutely necessary and many people who struggle with addiction will never overcome unless they find a Christian counselor who can help them work through some of the deeper mental struggles they may have. Education and counseling are key factors.

On a side bar here, please let me mention this. There are many people who feel called to ministry, because they want to reach and help people. There are far too few good, biblical Christian counselors. Everywhere I go I am pleading for good counselors to refer people to after my seminars. Not everyone called to ministry is called to be a pastor, please consider counseling or encouraging a young adult to take up the field of counseling.

3. **Accountability**—"Confess your trespasses to one another, and pray for one another, that you may be healed. The effective, fervent prayer of a righteous man avails much." —James 5:16

As with any sinful struggle, we absolutely need accountability partners. This is vital for porn users and even people simply dedicated to purity in relationships. We have to surround ourselves with people and influences that help us succeed. It is best, when dealing with a porn addiction, to choose one friend who you feel comfortable to go to in a time of temptation and stress; someone that will talk and pray with you any time of day. It can even be someone facing a similar struggle. There are some great internet accountability tools that utilize this step. They will install software that will send your accountability partner an email any time you search for or visit a website that is questionable. Your partner can give you a call and encourage you. If your marriage has been affected by porn use it's often best that your spouse is involved in the accountability process, but is not the main accountability partner—because of the level of involvement.

4. **Setting Boundaries**—"And if your eye causes you to sin, pluck it out and cast it from you. It is better for you to enter into life with one eye, rather than having two eyes, to be cast into hell fire." —Matthew 18:9

If the computer is too much of a temptation, get rid of it or install internet porn-blocking software. If you can't handle walking down the magazine aisle of the grocery store, have your wife get whatever you need from that aisle. This is why you need to be honest; to let someone help you see the bigger picture. Make sure someone holds you accountable and then execute the boundaries based on all these steps. Honesty is also crucial because we need to set our boundaries well before anything goes too far. Temptation can be like a charging bull, it gets moving and is hard to stop. Give him room! Set your boundaries far from the point of no return. Your friends, Scripture, and the Holy Spirit are the sources for great boundary setting.

To conclude this chapter, I would like to share with you the story of Gary. Gary stopped me in the hallway of an academy where I was presenting. He was the father of a student who was attending one of my seminars. Gary shared with me that he had battled porn use for nearly eleven years. He realized that he had a problem one day when he literally could not bring himself to have a sexual experience with his wife. She no longer seemed arousing to him. This struck him because he had always found her to be one of the most beautiful women he had ever met. This was weird and different. Late that same night, he found himself returning to the same internet site that he would go to almost every evening after his family went to bed. In that moment, he felt overwhelming shame and guilt. He was unable to be intimate with his beautiful wife, but was about to be intimate with a fake and disgusting video on the internet.

The next day he fought with the shame and guilt, yet through conviction he knew he must tell his wife. He confessed to her and they struggled for days to know what to do. They both felt ashamed and his wife felt as if her trust had been violated. Yet in the end she wanted to stay by him, and help him save their marriage. Gary decided to seek counseling, which his wife attended with him. He joined a men's group at church and found a friend he could trust. Gary made a covenant with God to pray three times a day for victory and freedom from lust, and addiction. This was the verse that he claimed three times a day,

> "For the grace of God that brings salvation has appeared to all men, teaching us that, denying ungodliness and worldly lusts, we should live soberly, righteously, and godly in the present age."
> —Titus 2:11, 12

After about four months of struggle, prayer, and sexual abstinence, everything started to come back to the life Gary knew before porn. Gary and his wife had rebuilt trust and intimacy through communication, and agreed upon boundaries (he literally did not go near a computer for nearly three months) and eventually they were able to enjoy a physical relationship again. He was attracted to his wife in a way that he never before had been, because now she had stood by him even though he had betrayed her trust. They had rebuilt their lives from the ashes of near destruction. Gary had to make a lot of difficult changes. But, as he stood there speaking with me, he told me it had been eighteen months since he was even tempted to watch porn. He had a new respect for his brothers in the church who had worked with him and had not pushed him away, but embraced him and helped him instead. He had worked with his pastor, weekly to receive encouragement and a prayer partner. He made sure he was the first one at prayer meeting every week. He felt he had gotten his life back. His was a story of redemption, forgiveness, and victory. Gary's story is one of thousands with similar outcomes. This story can be yours. This story can be an anthem for porn-free churches. God does heal and renew our minds. It's time we were honest about it, got help, were accountable to necessary people, and set boundaries.

> "Finally, brethren, whatever things are true, whatever things are noble, whatever things are just, whatever things are pure, whatever things are lovely, whatever things are of good report, if there is any virtue and if there is anything praiseworthy— meditate on these things." —Philippians 4:8

Chapter 10
The Grand Illusion

"You're a shooting star. I see a vision of ecstasy. When you hold me I'm alive, we're like diamonds in the sky" —Rihanna [32]

For my initial college education I attended a secular university. I was a baseball player and spent a lot of time around the team. On a team there are many different kinds of personalities, and lifestyles. One of the great temptations of playing baseball in a well-known college program is girls. Girls loved to hang around the team. Some of the guys I played with went on to have a professional career. Sadly, many girls thought that if they could snag one of these boys, then they would be the talk of the campus. Some would even settle for one night with these young men because, for a lifetime, they could say they were "loved" for one night by a future major leaguer.

These men knew that these girls thought this way and took advantage of it. One day after practice, one of the guys walked up to a group of girls hanging out at the practice field, and these were his exact words to one of them:

"Baby, did it hurt?" He asked.

"What do you mean?" She countered.

"Did it hurt when you fell from heaven cause you look like an angel!" he said with the most charming look on his face.

All the guys started laughing hysterically at our teammate's corny line. The shocking thing was that it worked! She started laughing and the guy actually left that day with her phone number. Knowing what that guy ultimately had in mind makes me feel sick to my stomach today. I feel so sorry for that girl. He used her for his pleasure and never spoke to her again. He had done this many times before.

---

32 Rihanna. *Diamonds*. Unapologetic. Written by Sia Furler. Stargate Productions, 2012.

He walked up to her, made eye contact with her, got close enough to speak to her directly and said those words. At that moment she felt something; something that she translated in her mind as intimacy and maybe, even love. She ended up giving her heart and body to him just to become a locker room rumor later that week. What makes people do such things?

On the other side of the coin are guys who actually think they have seen an angel, when looking at a particularly beautiful girl. Some people act like they have lost their minds over these new relationships. It's like an inexplicable power has taken them over, making them lose all control. Parents at times, think their children have gone crazy and no one can rescue them, it seems, from this intoxication.

In previous chapters, we have made the comparison of the gospel of romance being a type of anti-Christ. The Bible makes it clear that Satan is working with an end-time power and will use every means he can think of to overtake us. It says that false christs and false prophets will show up with false messages in the last days that will deceive even the very elect (Matthew 24:24).

Now the very elect aren't easily deceived. This deception must be so powerful, so overwhelming, that if minds are not tuned into the Holy Spirit they will be deceived. What could be so overwhelming?

The Bible says that there is a way that seems right to a man, but the end thereof are the ways of death. (Proverbs 16:25) What makes things "seem" right to us? Well, our mind makes decisions based on what we see, feel, touch, taste, and smell. Imagine what these senses must have experienced in Eden! But now what God has created for man's benefit the devil uses to deceive our minds. There is a close connection between the mind and body. What your mind thinks, you will do. What your body tells your mind to think, it often will. Is it possible that Satan will use our senses to deceive our minds?

Satan through the end time Beast will do great signs and wonders in the *sight* of men, even calling down fire from heaven (Revelation 13:13).

That verse is very interesting because it reminds me of Old Testament passages when God approved of a sacrifice and fire came from heaven to accept it; or God showing His great power by sending fire down from Heaven. (See 2 Kings 1, 2 Chronicles 7). These great deceptions must be so believable that it even seems like God is approving of whatever is happening, or even that his power is being shown through them. They are very deceptive indeed. The devil wants to use great overpowering things to convince and deceive our minds through our senses.

When Boy Meets Girl

One of the most overpowering experiences in the lives of human beings is when boy meets girl. What we are about to find out is that boy doesn't act girl crazy just because he's not very bright. It's because his senses have been stimulated, his mind reacts based on them.

Scientists have done a lot of research on what are called psychoactive substances, and their effects. In the 1980s, a psychiatrist named Michael Liebowitz did research into the underlying chemistry of "love sickness." What he suggested is that when boy meets girl or girl meets boy, that the body is capable of producing or emitting chemicals that are similar in structure to recreational and prescription drugs. Liebowitz believed that the initial rush of excitement that people associate with falling in love might be facilitated by brain chemistry that resembles stimulants like cocaine. Some of the calmness, or floating on air feelings is produced by brain chemicals that resemble narcotics like heroin, opium, or morphine. Other chemicals were likened to valium, and sedatives like barbiturates, alcohol and cannabis. Liebowitz also suggested that the enhanced state of beauty and heightened spiritual state that people report when they are "in love" might be ushered in by chemicals that resemble LSD, mescaline, and psilocybin.

Dr. Frank Tallis in his book *Love Sick: Love as a Mental Illness* states this, "One of the most important chemicals to be released when prospective lovers meet is phenyl ethylamine (or PEA); an amphetamine like compound that raises mood and hormones like adrenaline and noradrenalin which sharpens the senses. The potent cocktail of PEA and fight-flight hormones engenders a state of giddy excitement: and exhilarating 'rush.'[33]"

Tallis also goes on to say that a chemical very similar to PEA is found in none other than CHOCOLATE. This is why many people run to chocolate when stressed, or when a relationship has just ended. People often say that chocolate has similar chemicals that are released in the brain during sex. Actually chocolate has chemicals that people associate with feeling loved (I won't say another word about it, my fellow chocolate lovers).

---

33 Tallis, Frank. *Love-Sick: Love as a Mental Illness.* Pg. 221. New York, NY. Thunder's Mouth Press. 2004.

Now we can see why people are so vulnerable to making terrible decisions when relationships are first getting started, or when they are attracted to someone. This also explains why people are so vulnerable to the "rebound"; starting another relationship immediately after one ends. What is actually taking place is that we associate brain chemistry with "love" and when a relationship ends, we are like drug addicts experiencing withdrawals.

For centuries cultures have associated the effects of the senses on "love." Cologne commercials profess that a woman can fall in love with a man just by smelling him. Thousands of years ago women where relying on "love potions" to bring in a suitor. Today the cosmetics industry makes billions of dollars trying to make people look more desirable.

Again it seems that we have been deceived by the sexy beast. God created our senses as a way for us to interact with the newly created world. People today rely on the senses and their effects on the brain *to tell us what true love is.* How many of us have made a dumpster fire out of our love lives because we reduced love to mere chemical reactions; and we interpreted those chemicals to be love?

You've Been Warned

It shouldn't surprise us that this is happening. The Bible says this,

> "For men will be lovers of themselves, lovers of money, boasters, proud, blasphemers, disobedient to parents, unthankful, unholy, unloving, unforgiving, slanderers, without self-control, brutal, despisers of good." —2 Timothy 3:2, 3

In other words, people in the last days are like junkies; and in the context of our study about love, people are love junkies. We crave the experiences that will give us a rush of the brain drugs that we think are true love. As selfishness increases, so does the pursuit to be a pleasure seeker. Have you noticed that self-control is an endangered quality today? I believe that our youth are in the perfect storm of selfishness. Their desire for self-pleasure drives them to seek after the narcotics of the brain that their senses convince them are true love. The stress of the end times has them running to any source for love and peace. The media has their eyes, minds, and hearts in such a death grip that they feel that having self-control as part of their lives, is out of sync with the rest of society. Let's face it—love and sex are just plain fun. In these last days more than ever, people are drug and adrenaline junkies, and we are told that this is right.

I want to make one more connection with the adrenaline junkie in love illustration. In 1970, a research group in Vancouver did a study where they asked two groups of men to walk across two bridges. The first group walked across an ordinary safe bridge with all the safety measures clearly in place. The second group walked across a suspension bridge hundreds of feet in the air with very low rails and seemingly questionable safety measures. After each group walked their bridge individually they were approached by an attractive female researcher, and were encouraged to give her a call if they wanted to talk any more about the research in the near future. The men who walked across the suspension bridge were far more likely to give more sexualized answers on their post walk questionnaires and proved far more likely to give the female researcher a call. It seems that under stress and anxiety, lust and sexual attraction are increased, and are more likely to be acted upon.

By the way, much research has been done on numerous women who have actually fallen in love with—or felt sympathy—for a captor or someone who held them hostage in situations like a bank robbery. This tendency is not exclusive to men. It's known as the "Stockholm Syndrome" in the mental health field. It can happen to both men and women.

> "... knowing this first: that scoffers will come in the last days, walking according to their own lusts." —2 Peter 3:3

The last days actually make people more wicked. The stresses, cares, natural disasters, trials, influences of others and tribulations play on our senses and have an effect on our minds, actually making our sinfulness vulnerable to becoming even worse.

Many people have said that when they see the signs of the times coming upon them, then they will give their heart to Jesus. Not only does the Bible say this,

"Watch therefore, for you know neither the day nor the hour in which the Son of Man is coming." Matthew 25:13 but it seems that the days themselves will make it even more difficult to make a decision for Christ if we haven't already done so. This truth is clearly showing up in the lives of people in the church when it comes to love, lust, and sexuality. Too many are trying to cure the stress of the last days in sexual pleasure, and not in God and His word.

From the corny pick up line of my teammate to the old song *Earth Angel*, it is easily observed that there is a deeply ingrained belief that the people we love are somehow angelic, and heavenly.

"Beauty is certainly a soft, smooth, slippery thing, and therefore of a nature which easily slips in and permeates our souls." — Plato, *Lysis* [34]

"The power of a glance has been so much abused in love stories that it has come to be disbelieved in. Today, few people dare to say that two beings have fallen in love because they have looked at each other. Yet it is in this way that love begins, and in this way only." —Victor Hugo, *Les Misérables* [35]

"His voice is deep and gravelly. I once heard one of the girls say that he had the voice of a sex god, but because I've never really heard what a sex god sounds like, I can't verify that." —Melina Marchetta, *Saving Francesca* [36]

"I miss the sound of your voice … and I miss the rush of your skin and I miss the still of the silence as you breathe out I breathe in." —Matt Nathanson [37]

"Love is like the wind, you can't see it but you can feel it." — Nicholas Sparks, *A Walk to Remember* [38]

Our eyes see…

Our ears hear…

Our hands touch…

Our nose smells…

Our tongue tastes…

Our eyes become enchanted, our ears hear sweet love songs, our hands clasp together, sending out a rush of oxytocin (a brain bonding chemical). We smell the sweet aroma of perfume or cologne and all within us is convinced that this must be love. Every one of our senses proclaim without doubt that what we are experiencing is the purpose of our lives—love.

---

34   Plato, Loeb Classical Library; First Edition edition (January 1, 1925). Harvard University Press. Henderson, Jeffery editor. Cambridge MA.

35   Hugo, Victor. *Les Miserables*. Penguin Group. NY, NY. 1987. P. 956.

36   Marchetta, Melina. *Saving Francesca*. Random House Children's Books. NY, NY. 2003. P. 125

37   Nathanson, Matt. *Come on Get Higher*. Circle of Friends.Writers Matt Nathanson, Mark Weinberg, Vanguard Music, 2008.

38   Sparks, Nicholas, *A Walk to Remember*, Warner Books, New York, NY 1999.

This is like fire called down from heaven, an overwhelming deception that has consumed many at one time or another and lies waiting to devour our youth.

Not Just a Teenage Problem

While these feelings may be experienced at times by a godly husband and wife, these same feelings are not the definition of love. Yet many marriages have ended because they no longer feel the rush of these chemicals. The married couple feel that they have fallen out of love. While the fruit of true love is patience, society tells our hearts not to wait, but go for it. The fruit of true love is humility, yet our sinful minds feel exhilarated by self-indulgence. Conflict of the highest order.

> "The warfare against self is the greatest battle that was ever fought. The yielding of self, surrendering all to the will of God, requires a struggle; but the soul must submit to God before it can be renewed in holiness." [39]

This battle with self is not merely a struggle to make correct decisions. This is a battle to submit every one of our senses, every single thought, and every feeling to the Holy Spirit. This is a battle against the very chemistry of our bodies. This is a fight against everything we are told love is. In this battle, among the casualties there are often ruined marriages. This is a battle that will result in a person feeling out of sync with the world around him.

Guarded Hearts

Jesus says,

> "But seek first the kingdom of God, and His righteousness; and all these things shall be added to you." —Matthew 6:33

While the world is desperately seeking an emotional rush to make them feel loved, Jesus says that true love is only found in heaven. God tells us to seek Him first in all things and then all Godly things will be added to our lives. All things must pass through Him.

The Bible reminds us in various places to guard our hearts (Proverbs 4:23). There is an interesting passage that reads,

> "For those who sleep, sleep at night, and those who get drunk are drunk at night. But let us who are of the day be sober, putting

---

39   White, Ellen. *Steps to Christ.* Pg. 44. Nampa, Idaho. Pacific Press. 1892.

on the breastplate of faith and love, and as a helmet the hope of salvation. For God did not appoint us to wrath, but to obtain salvation through our Lord Jesus Christ." —1 Thessalonians 5:7–9

It is very interesting that, according to this verse, those called faithful and who are awake aren't "intoxicated" and guard their minds with the hope of salvation (the love of Jesus). Those that are looking forward to heaven, guard their hearts with the breastplate of faith, and true love. The Bible warns of a drunkenness of the world. As we have seen, there's enough in our own bodies to make us "drunk" without adding any extra chemicals like alcohol. This is why submitting every thought, feeling, and idea to the word of God is so important. It is our only safeguard against the great illusions that Satan uses against us.

Brain Development and Decision Making

Before we leave this chapter there is one more piece of brain development we need to discuss as it involves the growth and maturity of youth. Many of you have probably read about the development of the frontal lobe of the brain, as a person grows. This is the decision-making and self-control panel of the brain. Everything one does has to pass through this system. This all-important part of the brain is not fully developed in men until the age of 25, and women—between 18 and 20. Those of you, not familiar with this research probably just said to yourselves, "Oh that explains a lot!" when thinking about your son or daughter. Now consider the sexually charged media, peer pressure, and many other factors that are influencing the sexuality of young adults. There is already a tendency for us to be overcome with emotion when we are love-sick. Healthy adults often display symptoms of sociopathy, psychopathy, eating disorders, sleep disorders, waves of depression and highs of euphoria, obsession, compulsion, and other mental disturbances when they fall in love. Now take the brain chemistry issues discussed above, the reactions to those feelings that we just mentioned, and couple them with an immature decision making center of the brain. Is it any wonder that they often make poor decisions? The devil loves to destroy marriages before they ever happen by using this advantage over our youth. If he can destroy their sexual identity with their emotions and pile on baggage while they are young, he is overjoyed. This is why teaching and enforcing boundaries in sexuality and courtship are so important when kids are very young.

Setting a standard about how to associate with the opposite sex is key to their development later in life. It also helps them avoid vulnerable situations. It is both necessary to teach appropriate behavior around the opposite sex, and to set clear rules regarding dating behavior and friend-ships. These rules will pay off in a big way later in life. We must remem-ber it isn't enough to set a standard; we must be a standard. We must live out the principles we want our kids to make as part of their lives. Using Jesus as our example, who not only instructs us to overcome sin, but also did it Himself and gave us a pattern to follow. Words are not enough. I go into more detail about this all important strategy of setting boundaries in *The Gospel of Sex,* and *Love's Lies God's Replies.* We have to show our youth that the author of love also has the power to define love, and also commands how love should be acted out. This includes romance. Satan takes control of every mind that is not decidedly under the control of the Spirit of God.

If you still aren't convinced about how crazy people can be when it comes to the feelings of love, let me end this chapter with a true story that hap-pened to a person I met in a town near you.

There was a good looking, level-headed spiritual young man—we'll call him Sam. He goes on the internet and sees a friend of a friend on Facebook. This girl is gorgeous. He decides to send her a friend request. She accepts. They strike up a friendship and begin to private message each other. The private messages turn into long phone calls and eventu-ally Sam tells this girl that he loves her. Sam starts to buy her expensive things over the internet and she eventually tells Sam she loves him too. Soon Sam learns that she is in financial trouble, co-signs for a loan with her, and gives her his bank account information. At this point he has only ever seen online pictures of her and some grainy videos over Skype. Sam falls deeper and deeper in love with this beautiful girl and decides that he is going to hop on a plane and travel to her home and propose mar-riage. He gets to her home and a middle-aged woman opens the door. Sam asks for his girl, thinking this is her mom. To his horror, Sam learns that this middle-aged woman is the actual "girl" he had been talking to for all those months. She had used a fake picture for her profile and had been lying to Sam the entire time. He spent thousands of dollars on her, and was ready to propose marriage to someone he had never met face to face. Shocked and heart-broken, Sam returns home, still holding the picture of the woman from the internet photo in his hand; gazing at it as if still in love with her. Sam told me that it took him months to get over this imaginary girl. This story is too crazy to make up. More and more cunning people are intentionally taking advantage of love-starved people like Sam. A term has actually been coined, called "Catfishing."

How long will we allow our youth, friends, and church members to be trampled over by the Sexy Beast? People go crazy over love. We have become addicted to the chemical high of love-sickness. We have to tell and show people what true love is.

Chapter 11
Why the Church Hates Single People

I attended public high school. I can remember "those girls." They always seemed a bit dull and different. They didn't dress the same way as the other "hot" girls, and they didn't run around with the popular kids. They didn't go to parties and they didn't date around. They always seemed boring, and yet there was a part of me that wanted to be like them. They always seemed dignified and noble. In a way, I knew I *should* be like them, but I didn't know why.

I know why now. I found out later in life that they were Christian girls. Knowing them long after graduation, I see why they were the way they were. They dressed differently, and acted differently, because of their faith and parents' wishes. I know also why I secretly felt I should be like them. I myself was a Christian. I wanted to have Christian beliefs and hang out with the non-Christian kids. For me, head knowledge was enough. So in trying to identify with the cool kids I had to shun what those girls stood for. I didn't know them well enough to realize that what they were standing for was admirable and good. All I knew was that they were different. I never gave them the time of day.

The church often treats the single adults in our congregation in a similar way. Perhaps the title of the chapter was a bit extreme. We don't hate the single people, they just make us feel uncomfortable. Since they make us feel uncomfortable, singles get left out of church friendships (because married couples have a hard time spending time with singles); or we try to fix their singleness by getting them married, to allow them to fit in to the church culture better.

You know what I mean by fixing them. I literally saw it happen right in front of me once. I had just finished a seminar in a church in Michigan. A thirty-something year old man was asking me some questions, when all of a sudden there was an older lady tapping him on the shoulder. He turned around to see this older lady standing there with her hand firmly around a young woman's arm about his age. She had clearly manhandled her to talk to this guy. The older woman said,

"Danny, this is Megan—you know the one I've been telling you about. I thought after hearing Pastor's seminar, you might just want to meet her. You know you two aren't getting any younger! So Danny, this is Megan. Megan this is Danny. There, I've done my Godly service."

I kid you not, that is exactly how it happened. My face was just as red as Danny's and Megan's. They exchanged a few awkward words and I tried to cut the tension with some wit, but the awkwardness was so thick, we eventually laughed uncomfortably and walked away. The church has a really hard time with singleness. I have compiled a list of reasons why I believe we struggle with it so much; or some things I have heard people say about single people in the church.

1. **We want kids running around**—There is a huge amount of pressure for our young adults to get married and have kids. The reason for this is because many of our churches are missing young children. The pressure is on young adults to replenish the cute little babies and children's classes. What this actually creates is awkwardness and a schism between the single people and the church. They feel pressured; like they can't discuss their life with them. If they are struggling with something in their single life, they feel like there is no one that understands their situation.

2. **We love to play matchmaker**—Let's just face it… its fun! People love to take the credit for happily married couples. We can't fathom why attractive young men and attractive young ladies shouldn't be together.

3. **There are rumors about them**—I have heard it a number of times. "We can't figure out why Johnny is not married. He's good looking, has a great job, and is active in the church. Some people wonder if he is … gay." For some reason, in the minds of some church members, people who are not married are weird. It's not just homosexuality that is often rumored. Sometimes they speculate of relationships with people who are not Christians or that they're mental eunuchs. We have a hard time accepting that someone may just be happy and content at the moment just being single.

4. **They think you are missing out**—Another reason that the church has a hard time relating to singles is that, because we

enjoy our spouses and kids, we believe somehow they are missing out on life if they are not married. It's not until recently that the church has begun to teach that being single is a God-given privilege.

5. **It's uncomfortable for them** (they feel awkward). Because of the way our society is structured, people are getting married later in life. The average age for marriage is twenty-five. Often people from the previous generation have a hard time relating to the changes of the current culture. In my parent's generation, people got married as teenagers, so seeing people who are in their late twenties and early thirties who are unmarried is just plain different for them. Many people who are in their late fifties and older never had to go to college to obtain a career; not so with today's generation. There is a much different experience between the generations.

6. **They don't know any better, they were never told.** As we have previously stated in this book, for many there is a close association between marriage and family, and perceived success in life and strong gender identity. People believe what makes you a man is your wife and kids; or what makes you a woman are your mothering skills. Interestingly enough, Paul has something much different to say about single people.

"For I wish that all men were even as I myself. But each one has his own gift from God, one in this manner and another in that. But I say to the unmarried and to the widows: It is good for them if they remain even as I am." —1 Corinthians 7:7, 8.

There is some debate among Bible scholars about whether or not Paul was married at some point in his life. It was a requirement of the Pharisees to be married. Paul was a Pharisee, so some Bible scholars believe that he either somehow got around the rule, or as the above verse implies, that he was a "widow." Paul's wife could have either died at some point before his conversion or left him because of his Christianity. Either way, Paul clearly says here that it is in fact good to remain single. Now this is much different than most of the messages we hear about marriage in the church. We not only encourage marriage, we expect it.

Many times in his writings, Paul relates a person's worth, not to their marital status, but to their engagement in God's work. In fact, he makes the case that people who are single can actually achieve more for God—which in Paul's mind is the duty of man.

"But I want you to be without care. He who is unmarried cares for the things of the Lord—how he may please the Lord." —1 Corinthians 7:32

"Therefore we make it our aim, whether present or absent, to be well pleasing to Him. For we must all appear before the judgment seat of Christ, that each one may receive the things *done* in the body, according to what he has done, whether good or bad. Knowing, therefore, the terror of the Lord, we persuade men; but we are well known to God, and I also trust are well known in your consciences." —2 Corinthians 5:9–11 (emphasis supplied)

In order to truly appreciate single people we must remember what marriage is not.

Marriage is not a person's identity.

Marriage is not a person's greatest hope.

Marriage is not where we find true peace and happiness.

Marriage is not supposed to be the most important relationship for mankind.

Marriage is not required.

So what is the problem with being single? The answer is nothing. What the church must do is realize the great asset we have in our single people. We must stop trying to fix them up in a human relationship and remember that their relationship with Jesus should be the aim of the church. By strengthening their relationship with Jesus and giving them opportunities to serve God, they might just meet a spouse (but that is not the main focus of the church). Now don't get me wrong, at times introducing people in a friendly way is a positive thing, but playing match maker is not our divine calling.

I began this chapter talking about the weird Christian girls in my school growing up. I knew that somehow I should have been like them. In a way I believe the church, deep down, feels like that they should be like the singles among us. Many of them are truly dedicated totally to God, and genuinely have the dedication to God that we all realize we should. For many married people this is convicting. We know we should be as dedicated to the service of God as some of these non-married folks, so rather than helping them grow close to God, we try to make them like us, married and more distracted from the work of God.

Actually in Bible prophecy we are given a convicting symbol:

"Then I looked, and behold, a Lamb standing on Mount Zion, and with Him one hundred *and* forty-four thousand, having His Father's name written on their foreheads. And I heard a voice from heaven, like the voice of many waters, and like the voice of loud thunder. And I heard the sound of harpists playing their harps. They sang as it were a new song before the throne, before the four living creatures, and the elders; and no one could learn that song except the hundred *and* forty-four thousand who were redeemed from the earth. These are the ones who were not defiled with women, for they are virgins. These are the ones who follow the Lamb wherever He goes. These were redeemed from *among* men, *being* firstfruits to God and to the Lamb. And in their mouth was found no deceit, for they are without fault before the throne of God." —Revelation 14:1–5 (emphasis supplied)

The 144,000 are some of the most fascinating and admired people in all Bible prophecy. People who live in the very last days before Jesus comes, want to be in this group of people who will be translated and never see death. Notice the Bible refers to them as male "virgins." This is a symbol that has to do most specifically with their dedication only to Jesus, contrasting them with the harlot of Revelation 18 who is the symbol of every selfish and confused version of religion. While the reference to this group as virgins is not specifically about their sexual history, it does actually deal with their sexuality. This group follows Jesus (the Lamb) wherever He goes. In other words, they do the will of Jesus no matter what. They love Jesus and only Jesus. This *could* include married people, but in fact they are in heart, mind and life at this time *only* married to Jesus. In this time they are doing what Paul refers to:

"Do not deprive one another *except with consent for a time, that you may give yourselves to fasting and prayer.*" —1 Corinthians 7:5 (emphasis supplied)

Because of the world's condition at this time, human relationships are all filtered through an end time faith in Jesus. The 144,000 realize that He is the fulfillment of their heart. Single people today can be symbols of the 144,000. While the church has in the past focused too much on getting them married to someone else, we should have been focused on helping them dedicate their hearts *only* to Jesus. Marriage is far less significant, but by helping them know Jesus, we could actually be preparing them for marriage.

Single and Proud of It

I met Mary in New Jersey. Mary marched right up to me one day after my morning sermon at her church. I had just finished a message much like the one in this chapter. With a smile on her face she said:

> "Thank you so much. I am 75 years old and have never been married a day in my life. I have gone on eleven overseas mission trips, started a health evangelism outreach nearby, and all my life people have been trying to marry me off. I feel called to be single. Sure, there has been a man or two over the years I've had some interest in, but I just never felt called to get married. I get more out of service to my God than I believe I ever could from getting married. I have never understood why everyone always thought I should get married. I understand why people get married and think it's beautiful, but I never felt it was right for my life. Spreading the Gospel is the most important thing in my life and I get no greater satisfaction than when I am doing that."

Mary left a huge smile on my face. She was vibrant, happy, strong and healthy. I distinctly remember thinking that I certainly want grandchildren, but if my daughters grow up to make the same life decisions as Mary, I would be a very proud father. In the same way, we need to be a church that is proud of its single people who dedicate their lives to Jesus. In a way we are all called to be single; single in our dedication to Jesus. Our relationship with Him is the basis for every relationship we could have. Our relationship with Him will have an influence on how we conduct our life, and how intimate we can become with others. If we keep Jesus at a distance, we will keep others at a distance; and that includes our spouse.

Chapter 12
Virginity and the Great Controversy

ast year I overheard a conversation among college students that I won't soon forget. They were having a debate using their Bibles about the difference between adultery and fornication. One young lady had an especially strong opinion, "Adultery and fornication are the same thing, they happen when people are married and have sex with someone that is not their spouse." At first I was astounded at her wisdom. I too believe that adultery and fornication is essentially the same thing as I will explain below. As I kept listening to this girl, however, I realized that she was not nearly as wise as I had thought. She went on, "So, if you're not married, there is no such thing as the sin of fornication."

I immediately interrupted the conversation.

It is astounding how the Bible is being used today. There is such biblical illiteracy that people are literally making it say anything they feel like it should say. I have a hard time fighting my frustration when I hear a politician say that the Bible is pro-slavery, or against gay people. The truth is that the Bible is a revelation of true love, not a book of various opinions.

Fidelity Now and Later

Adultery and fornication *is* the same thing. In my seminars I break it down this way: Adultery involves marriage, fornication involves someone who likely will be married someday. If you are committing fornication outside of marriage, you are actually committing adultery with someone else's future spouse, and committing adultery on your own future spouse. On a much grander scale, fornication and sexual sin is actually adultery against God Himself.

In scripture, God's people are repeatedly referred to as His bride,

"Do not fear, for you will not be ashamed; Neither be disgraced, for you will not be put to shame; For you will forget the shame

of your youth, And will not remember the reproach of your widowhood anymore. For your Maker is your husband, The LORD of hosts is His name; And your Redeemer is the Holy One of Israel; He is called the God of the whole earth. For the LORD has called you Like a woman forsaken and grieved in spirit, Like a youthful wife when you were refused, says your God."
—Isaiah 54:4–6

Anytime in the Bible when God's people ran to any other source for protection, peace, safety, happiness, worship, money, or identity, God called it adultery or fornication.

"Then I saw that for all the causes for which backsliding Israel had committed adultery, I had put her away and given her a certificate of divorce; yet her treacherous sister Judah did not fear, but went and played the harlot also." —Jeremiah 3:8

"You also committed harlotry with the Egyptians, your very fleshly neighbors, and increased your acts of harlotry to provoke Me to anger." —Ezekiel 16:26

"For out of the heart proceed evil thoughts, murders, *adulteries*, fornications, thefts, false witness, blasphemies" —Matthew 15:19 (emphasis supplied)

The amazing thing about God is that even though His people continuously ran to other sources for their well-being and worship, He ceaselessly called them back to Him and desired to accept them as His bride again. The book of Hosea is filled with this wonderfully romantic message. Consider this passage from a God who is desperately trying to win back the hearts of people who have forgotten their True Love.

"Therefore, behold, I will allure her, and bring her into the wilderness, and speak tenderly to her. … And there she shall answer as in the days of her youth, as at the time when she came out of the land of Egypt. "And in that day, declares the LORD, you will call me 'My Husband,' and no longer will you call me 'My Baal.' For I will remove the names of the Baals from her mouth, and they shall be remembered by name no more. And I will make for them a covenant on that day with the beasts of the field, the birds of the heavens, and the creeping things of the ground. And I will abolish the bow, the sword, and war from the land, and I will make you lie down in safety. And I will betroth you to me forever. I will betroth you to me in *righteousness* and in justice, in steadfast love and in mercy. I will betroth you to me in *faithfulness*. And you shall know the LORD." —Hosea 2:14–20 (emphasis supplied)

Look at those gorgeous words, *righteousness* and *faithfulness*. It is out of love that God desires to restore us; no matter what has happened. According to Hosea it is also no matter how many times we have been unfaithful in our relationship with Him. He is willing to call us righteous and faithful even though we have not been anything close to it. It is by His decree, by the decision of our heart, and our desire for forgiveness that He provides restoration.

The Harlot Versus the Bride

In previous chapters we have identified sexuality as a false religion and a false gospel, promising hope. Our sexual choices reflect what we believe saves us. Are we more faithful to our feelings and passions or to the God who satisfies our every longing? The trouble is that we have all gone astray. All of us have run to another lover, literally or spiritually. We have been defiled by the things of this world through our selfish choices about sex, money, entertainment, stewardship and every other area of life. In the last chapter we mentioned the pure 144,000 in the book of Revelation. They stand in contrast to the "Great Prostitute" of Revelation 17.

> "So he carried me away in the Spirit into the wilderness. And I saw a woman sitting on a scarlet beast which was full of names of blasphemy, having seven heads and ten horns. The woman was arrayed in purple and scarlet, and adorned with gold and precious stones and pearls, having in her hand a golden cup full of abominations and the filthiness of her fornication. And on her forehead a name was written: MYSTERY, BABYLON THE GREAT, THE MOTHER OF HARLOTS AND OF THE ABOMINATIONS OF THE EARTH. I saw the woman, drunk with the blood of the saints and with the blood of the martyrs of Jesus. And when I saw her, I marveled with great amazement." —Revelation 17:3–6

She is called the Great Prostitute because she is a symbol of every religion that is not centered on Christ and grace-based salvation through faith. In a way, she is a great symbol of every one of us. Some of us are filled with the worship of self-righteousness, idols, sex, porn, companionship, career, etc. Another symbol in Revelation that contrasts with the prostitute is the pure woman in Revelation 12, clothed in white, light and purity. So this presents a dilemma. How can this symbol of the church be described as "pure" when it is filled with people that are anything but pure? The pure woman from Revelation 12 is a symbol of the bride, God's people. Her purity is her faith, and her dedication to God's word. Ironically, she is made up of believers who have been called by God 'adulterers' in the past. If this is true, God must be in the business of taking adulterers and making them pure. So all of us stand wondering, is there any way for someone who has been impure to be made pure again?

> "For I am jealous for you with godly jealousy. For I have betrothed you to one husband, that I may present you as a chaste *virgin* to Christ." —2 Corinthians 11:2 (emphasis supplied)

Thankfully, the answer to this question is, yes. According to Paul, not only are we God's people and by faith accepted back after sin, but He also calls us a 'virgin'. This is such a powerful truth. In fact, it is this pathway from sin to victorious purity that God uses as the shining example of His love in the battle between good and evil.

> "And I said to him, "Sir, you know." So he said to me, "These are the ones who come out of the great tribulation, and washed their robes and made them white in the blood of the Lamb." —Revelation 7:14

Of these people God says

> "He who overcomes shall inherit all things, and I will be his God and he shall be My son." —Revelation 21:7

To every abused little girl, God is calling you, through faith, to be his pure undefiled bride. To every young man who has slept with his girlfriend, God is calling you to be clothed with purity and to be one of His people. To every literal prostitute on the streets today, God is calling you to be his pure virgin bride. You see, what troubles God most and makes Him jealous is not only what we have done and what has happened to us, but what our religion is; where our faith is. Is ours a religion of fear? Guilt? Selfishness? Lust? Pride? Indulgence? If we are trying to be loved, and feel loved through this kind of religion, we are giving our hearts to another husband and committing adultery. If our heart and mind are filled with a religion other than the pure religion of Jesus, it crowds out the very one who is trying to forgive us and make us new. God is saying to all of us,

"And I said to her, 'You shall stay with me many days; you shall not play the harlot, nor shall you have a man—so, too, will I be toward you.'" —Hosea 3:3.

Purity Restored

When we give ourselves to Him and only Him, He calls us His pure, chaste, bride. Being a "spiritual virgin" is less about what has happened before, than it is about what is happening right now. Who or what has your heart this moment? Does the shame of your past hold you down? What is on your television right now? When you are intimate with your spouse, is the experience more about your own pleasure than it is about what you share together? Do you try to find peace and safety in the arms of lovers, or by looking at your bank account, or by the size of your home? What is in your heart this moment?

Fidelity to our spouses is about choosing not to look lustfully at others, by bouncing our eyes away from a temptation. Fidelity is about a choice each moment. Each moment we are choosing whether or not to be a good husband or wife. Each moment we are choosing whether or not to be devoted to Jesus. What kind of person are you allowing God to make you moment by moment? Are you letting Him prepare you to be a good husband or wife someday if you are single? Faithfulness to God is a day-to-day, moment by moment relationship. It's the same for our faithfulness to God. Are you more like the prostitute who has filled her life with every other religion than the one centered on Jesus? Just as that impure woman reflects impurity clothed with the symbols of false religion, our lives reflect where our heart is.

Are you part of the statistics?

Are you one of the men who has had 15 or more lovers?

Are you one of the 20% of women in the church with a porn problem?

Are you in an exclusive, yet out of wedlock sexual relationship?

Are you so desperate to find 'true love' that God's word and the advice of faithful people around you have little impact?

If you can say 'yes' to these questions, you are falling prey to the false religion. Your heart is being filled with a false peace and hope that will eventually lead to more pain. You are the one God is calling back to be made pure. God wants to make us the kind of people where Jesus lives in our hearts every moment. What a loving God He really is!

"These are the ones who were not defiled with women, for they are virgins. These are the ones who follow the Lamb wherever He goes. These were redeemed from among men, being firstfruits to God and to the Lamb." —Revelation 14:4.

Right now, in this moment, who or what lives in your heart? Those who love Jesus follow Him wherever He goes. We are willing to leave every other lover that this world offers, and be betrothed only to Him. If your heart is filled with Jesus, He calls you his beautiful, pure, virgin. In this sense even married people are called to be His 'virgins'. These are those whose hearts are sealed with His Holy Spirit through a faithful relationship. Married or unmarried, God wants us as His faithful bride.

Sexual Sin Leads to Spiritual Adultery.

I'll never forget her face. My wife and I stood visiting with a number of teenage young ladies after a youth meeting one morning. She looked older than the rest of the group, maybe in her early twenties. It's not uncommon for young adults to sneak into the teen meetings when they hear what we will be studying. She was ready to cry, not out of sorrow as much as resolve. You could see it in her face. That day we had been talking about boundaries, and at the end of the meeting, I said a special prayer for those whose boundaries had been violated without their consent— the sexually abused. My wife had specifically prayed with the group that day. She prayed for peace and resolve to settle upon their hearts as part of the closing prayer. I could see that this girl wanted to talk to us about something from her past, just by the look on her face. I said a final goodbye to the group we were casually visiting with and excused myself to talk with her. My wife joined me soon after.

As soon as she made eye contact with Kelly, she started to cry. Through her tears she said that my wife's prayer had touched her heart in a special way. She had been abused as a young girl and since that time she had one sexual relationship after another to try and feel loved. This is not uncommon for people who have experienced abuse. The reason being, they often feel used and worthless, and try to find their worth through sexual attention and intimacy. I was so glad Kelly was with me that day because she grabbed this girl in her arms and let her cry out her pain. After she was finished crying, she said that she was not crying for her past, but was crying because she needed help in her future. She had realized that day that she was trying to find peace through sex. At that moment she was making her commitment to not allow her abuser to affect her sexuality anymore. This courageous young woman realized that trying to mask her pain with sexual relationships was not allowing her to deal with the scars from her past. She told us that she wanted to make a decided change. She wanted to experience true healing in Jesus and wanted to stop the vicious cycle of sexual sin in her life. She had been robbed of her boundaries, but now she wanted to live by them. These tears that were now drying on her face were tears of resolve. She truly wanted to follow the Lamb wherever He goes. We talked to her about the great value God places on her life and helped her identify some immediate steps she could take. Then we had prayer and helped her choose an accountability partner she could trust. Today, she is truly a daughter of God like Mary Magdalene, like the Samaritan woman at the well, like Rahab. Pure, not from what she had done, but pure because Jesus had made her that way. He promises to help her, and everyone like her, stay true to Him.

Sexual virgins or not, we are all called to the purity of faith. This young lady had believed in the religion of sexuality as her savior, when truly it was her destroyer. There is a Healer. His name is Jesus and His presence in our lives makes us pure, undefiled, and faithful. Choose purity moment by moment. Choose Jesus moment by moment and you certainly will live as He desires for you.

Chapter 13
Companion

"Behold, the virgin shall be with child, and bear a Son, and they shall call His name Immanuel," which is translated, "God with us." —Matthew 1:23

We are living in a truly unprecedented era. In past decades for example, athletes were judged based on their entire body of work—over their whole career. Now, because of social media, public opinion can sway back and forth about them with every shot, or at bat. It used to be that the only time people followed what was happening in current events was during the 6 o'clock news or with their morning newspaper. Now Twitter zings out public opinion faster than you can say 'World Wide Web'.

Every time a celebrity steps out of their home, their picture is taken and people begin to scrutinize their fashion style and demeanor. Information and opinion move faster than ever before. There are now twenty-four hour news programs. Social media and the internet have literally changed the world. It would be foolishness to not realize that it has changed society and even our individual identities. It has become who we are.

People are now texting during funerals and weddings. Businessmen post to Facebook during meetings. People check Twitter during church. Teenagers will text each other while sitting in the same room with each other! People literally sleep with their phones and iPads. In many ways, a person's online identity is more real and important to them than their actual literal day to day life. People believe that texting, and posting to social media actually creates real relationships, almost an "I share therefore I am" mindset; thinking that the little snippets of Facebook "likes" and "re-tweets" are actually a sign that people really care.

While we are sharing more than ever, we actually are hiding from each other more than ever. Social media allows us to create for ourselves an identity that is specifically designed to encourage people to "like" us. Due to the tendency to crave real intimacy, many people have created an online version of themselves that is highly edited, and seldom real. This edited self is subject only to popular opinion, or what will create the most attention. Ironically even though people may share a status, or like a post, they only have to think about you for a few seconds. Still people today thrive on how many "likes" a post will get or how many "re-tweets" their followers will create based on their original messages. More than ever today, a person derives his or her self-worth based on the statistics of a machine, or a few sentences of response written by a near stranger on their social media posts. People will edit themselves more and more because we have been taught that the more hits your website gets, or views your YouTube channel receives, or followers your Facebook page has, the more people value you. We have become consumerists when it comes to caring about people. The better one does at creating a 'brand' for themselves, the better chance at fake online fame. So in order to feel valued, people will retouch their image and identity to make liking them easier. This becomes evident when people make vague posts like "so sad," or "I can't believe this," without any other details. These posts are some of the clearest examples of people just hoping and wishing that someone will respond with a caring "what's wrong?" or "Oh, I'm so sorry." Often it doesn't even matter *who* is responding but just that *someone* is responding. *While we are seeking attention, what is actually happening is that we are expecting more from technology and less from each other.* This reality shows a great cry for help from society for real and authentic intimacy. This kind of intimacy is difficult and messy, which challenges our selfishness and creates transformation that is uncomfortable. Intimacy with others has become little nuggets of time here and there, so that we will feel less alone. We desire intimacy from others, but we are increasingly uncomfortable with working at intimacy with someone else. People sit together in a waiting room and rather than dealing with the uncomfortable feeling of talking with a new person, they will pull out their smartphone to check on their online community.

Thus identity is based solely on public opinion. This begins to chip away at our ability for self-reflection and quiet self-examination through the guidance of the Holy Spirit. People have even begun to change who they are in real life based on their online edited personality. They spend hours daily advertising themselves with posts and tweets. In this way this generation is the product of the media.

I will never forget a teenager who I personally knew and had 'friended' on Facebook. I noticed that she had changed her profile from "interested in guys" to a description that would be defined as bisexual. I asked her about it and she said that she really wasn't bisexual but it was the cool thing to do on the internet with a few of her friends and actually got her a bunch more Facebook friends, (Ha Ha, she laughed). Later that same year, I learned that she had actually experimented with a bisexual lifestyle because as she put it, "it sounded interesting." Her real life had been transformed by her online identity. A few months later she came to me privately and stated that she wished she had never tried out the "bisexuality thing," but in a way was glad she did, because she met a lot of really interesting new friends.

If there were ever a time for parents to monitor the online activity of their kids, its today. Using internet accountability software, and scheduling regular internet black out times, families have literally saved their relationships and communication with one another.

The Search For Certainty

Rather than allowing God to define us and bring us true intimacy, we believe that our lifestyle and especially our social media activity will make it so we never have to be alone. Social media has literally changed our very minds and the way we look at life. I recently read an article that stated that Facebook is being cited as a reason for divorce on a surprisingly large percentage of divorce filings. More and more people are receiving attention from former lovers, or new lovers and are having real life or online affairs. It seems that even the computer can drive up those lovesick drugs in our brains that make us think we are missing out on Eden. Maybe that attention from a former lover can make us feel completely happy and content.

In her 2012 TED talk "Connected, But Alone[40]," Psychologist Dr. Sherri Turkle was sharing her research on this very topic. She had been at the forefront in the early 90's promoting the wonderful advancements in technology that allowed people to instant message each other, send emails, and connect with each other on a level never seen before.

"The advantage then," Turkle says, was that "people could connect with each other, and then unplug from it. Now people nearly never unplug."

---

40   Turkle, Sherry. Feb. 2012. *Connected But Alone*. Retrieved from: http://www.ted.com/talks/ sherry_turkle_alone_together.html.

Her concern is that this connectedness is actually not creating healthier minds, personalities, and people, but actually destroying our ability to be intimate with each other, and genuinely communicate. In fact, many experts have noted that heavy users of social media report less satisfaction with life, and a greater likelihood of depression. It seems that as social media draws us inward with our focus, the less happy we actually are. We were made for relationships, and the more self-centered we become, the less happy we are. People are desperate for relationships; to give and receive intimacy. It seems that our efforts in social media have become terribly misguided and are a dead end.

In another part of her presentation, Dr. Turkle relates an amazing, yet heart-wrenching story based on her research. It demonstrates how easily people will bond with machines because of a great desire for empathy and companionship. In her research, Turkle presented a study about elderly people who were given robotic animals to live with. Very quickly these elderly people began to speak to the robotic animals which had the ability to respond verbally to them. Their conversations progressed from the novelty of speaking to a talking seal, for example, to intimate conversation about their loneliness and personal pain. It seems that human beings want someone, anyone, to love and be intimate with.

God With Us

My wife and I love to walk through cemeteries. (I know that is a very awkward transition at this point, but stay with me here). A few years ago, on a large number of gravestones, I noticed a symbol that I became curious about. The symbol was a cross and an anchor that were interlocking. Others had simply a sole anchor sculpted on the top of them. I was intrigued by this and started doing some research. As it turns out, the Anchor is an ancient Christian symbol. During the first century, the Christian symbol that was most associated with Christians was not the cross, but the anchor. By using this symbol we see that the first century Christians understood an important part of the ministry of Jesus on behalf of man.

> "That by two immutable things, in which it was impossible for God to lie, we might have a strong consolation, who have fled for refuge to lay hold upon the hope set before us: Which hope we have as an anchor of the soul, both sure and steadfast, and which entereth into that within the veil; Whither the forerunner is for us entered, even Jesus, made an high priest for ever after the order of Melchizedek." —Hebrews 6:18–20.

This is a very powerful passage. The early Christian church understood from scripture that Jesus, after His resurrection and ascension, began a work on behalf of His children as the book of Hebrews states. This work, they believed was their hope. The Bible states that Jesus became a High Priest and began to be our intercessor before the Father. What an amazing "hope"! Hope is a word that is tossed out there too lightly these days. For many, hope is nothing more than positive thinking. People say things like "well, let's hope for the best," but the hope for a Christian is much more than positive thinking. Hope for those who believe in Jesus, is steadfast anticipation of a promise; meaning an imminent reality. This promise that the book of Hebrews is referring to is the truth that Jesus is acting as our mediator, our intercessor, and our High Priest in Heaven. This work for us is what anchors us to the Father.

When an anchor is thrown into the water, it is because the crew doesn't want the ship to drift away. It may move a little here and there, but with the anchor firmly in place that boat cannot be lost. This anchor is the lifeline between humanity and heaven. It is our connection. Jesus taught this powerful truth when He said this to His disciples:

> "Nevertheless, I tell you the truth. It is to your advantage that I go away; for if I do not go away, the Helper will not come to you; but if I depart, I will send Him to you." —John 16:7

> "In Him you also *trusted,* after you heard the word of truth, the gospel of your salvation; in whom also, having believed, you were sealed with the *Holy Spirit* of promise, who is the *guarantee* of our inheritance until the redemption of the purchased possession, to the praise of His glory." —Ephesians 1:13, 14

The hope of the Christian includes help. This help from heaven is an assured promise. Jesus said that it was good that He should go away, because it would be to the benefit of man. How could Jesus' leaving be to our benefit? Jesus knew that as He was in heaven working on our behalf, the Holy Spirit would come with His comforting, convicting, transformative power. Jesus could live *with* us, but the Holy Spirit can live *in* us. This close union of God dwelling in our hearts assures us that the Gospel unites those who love God with Him in an eternal intimacy.

The Father is the Rock of life and love in heaven. Jesus is the Anchor that keeps us firmly attached to the Rock, and the Holy Spirit is the line that attaches us to the Anchor. The ministry of Jesus on our behalf in Heaven allows us to truly be connected with the Father. Because of this we are never alone. Because of the Rock, the Anchor, and the Line, we never have to worry if someone isn't there for us. While we are living in the struggles and trials of life, we have an Anchor that holds us fast to heaven. The most wonderful part is that, as we are attached to heaven, we get transformed into a citizen of heaven. The Holy Spirit is the part of the Godhead that works in cooperation with the ministry of Jesus in heaven. As we crave love and are shown love from God in His word and power, we become transformed into heaven's definition of love. Jesus anchors us to the Father. This is an eternal relationship; an oneness between God and man. God's image is renewed in man as The Godhead works to connect and restore fallen man to Himself through the work of the Father, Son, and Holy Spirit.

> "Create in me a clean heart, O God, and renew a steadfast spirit within me. Do not cast me away from Your presence, and do not take Your Holy Spirit from me. Restore to me the joy of Your salvation, and uphold me *by Your* generous Spirit." —Psalm 51:10–12

> "Then I will give them a heart to know Me, that I *am* the LORD; and they shall be My people, and I will be their God, for they shall return to Me with their whole heart." —Jeremiah 24:7

When you are tempted—remember the lifeline.

When you are feeling lonely—remember the Anchor.

When you want to know what to do—remember the Rock that will not let you drift away.

When you need victory over sin—Remember that you are connected with the indwelling Holy Spirit, which allows you to communicate with Jesus, who goes right to the Father on our behalf. We are always attached to Eternal Power and love.

The love of heaven is a selfless, unconditional love, so the work of Jesus not only is a work *of* love; it is a work in order for us *to* love. People believe that by falling in love with a lover, they will find love. In reality, by giving our heart to Jesus, He transforms us into love, into His image. We cannot have true intimacy with any human being without intimacy with Christ through the Holy Spirit.

The Bible states this:

"Now by this we know that we know Him, if we keep His commandments. He who says, "I know Him," and does not keep His commandments, is a liar, and the truth is not in him. But whoever keeps His word, truly the love of God is perfected in him. By this we know that we are in Him. He who says he abides in Him ought himself also to walk just as He walked."
—1 John 2:3–6

A sign of our relationship with Jesus is that He is living in our hearts and the natural result of this relationship is that our lives are in harmony with Him, keeping His commandments, and loving as He loved. The work of Jesus gifts us with the ability to speak directly to God. He wants to talk with us. He wants to communicate His plans and His dreams for our lives. The cries for intimacy that so many people post to social media should actually be silent prayers to our Father in Heaven. Deciding on a lifestyle based on public opinion is self destructive and sinful; the exact opposite of the kind of relationship that Jesus' ministry as our Anchor in Heaven has made for us. Sins and struggles, failures and praises can go directly to God through our tight relationship with the God of the Universe. He cares, He listens, He saves, He provides, He protects. What more could we want?

This promise is especially valid for the days we are living in:

"… For He Himself has said, 'I will never leave you nor forsake you.'" —Hebrews 13:5.

"Let those who fear the Lord now say, 'His mercy *endures* forever.'

I called on the Lord in distress; The Lord answered me *and set me* in a broad place.

The LORD *is* on my side; I will not fear. What can man do to me?"
—Psalm 118:4–6 (emphasis supplied)

"… I am with you always, *even* to the end of the age." —Matthew 28:20

It seems that Jesus was especially concerned with reminding us of His companionship with us even at the end of time. As the world around us is riddled with selfishness, self worship, insecurity and lustful pursuits like in the days of Noah, God wants us to remember that Jesus' High Priestly ministry in heaven is working to combat the evil that is in the world. As we struggle with sin and despair, by using God's promises, we can know that our bodies are the temple of the Holy Spirit (1 Corinthians. 6:19) and we are not our own. We have been bought by Him. When we need victory over addictions, the Holy Spirit reminds us,

"For whatever is born of God overcomes the world. And this is the **victory** that has overcome the world—our faith" (1 John 5:4). As the world around us gets filthier, the ministry of the Godhead cleanses us and works through us to overcome temptation and trials. It is through this intimacy that God achieves the restoration of His nature in man, that we may walk with Him every day as He originally intended at Adam's creation by His own hand. He will not cease to be our constant companion.

Testimony of True Love

As I sat there in their living room, I couldn't help but feel at home. It wasn't because it looked like my house—their well kept furniture still had the pale hues, characteristic of the early 1990s when they had been purchased. My furniture has the wear of a young family from a house filled with noisy kids. Their home was peaceful and serene with walls bearing the pictures of grown children and grand children they adore. I didn't feel at home with this couple because of a similar history or because our lives had all that much in common. I felt at home there because I could sense God's presence. The same God I love, lived in that home.

This couple had been long time church members. I was there because the man of the house had been recently diagnosed with stage four colon cancer and was only given a few weeks to live. As I sat there visiting with them, I grew more comfortable sitting and relaxing on the sofa just watching them and listening to them talk. Even though this couple would soon be parted by death after being together for nearly 65 years, there was more smiling and laughter in that room than in my own home filled with happy little children. There were tears, but they were not of sadness. The tears rolling from our eyes were made by the laughter from happy days past. I was the one benefiting from this "pastoral" visit. Today, they were the ones pastoring me. What touched me most was the way that they looked at each other—not with the fiery passion that romantic films show. Every time their eyes met, there was deep respect and admiration. This was a gaze of two people who knew each other's stories, each other's weaknesses, and each other's good times. They knew these moments because they had shared most of them together. They had been together through their young adulthood, child rearing years, and now old age. There had hardly been a day that they had been apart.

He had always been a man who treated his wife like a queen, constantly speaking well of her and catering to her every need. She always looked at him like he was the greatest man she had ever met. The fire that existed in this marriage was not from heated passion; it was the fire of holiness, and deepest appreciation for one another. These two had the kind of marriage that garnered respect and attention from others. People at church often gushed over their marriage in public. Everyone agreed that there was something special about these two. As I think of that visit, I still feel great warmth from being in that home that evening. I could sense the love that existed between them. They had laughed, loved, fought battles together, and had an entire lifetime—a great legacy left behind with no regrets.

That night, before leaving, I had to ask them something. I felt compelled to ask them what had kept them together for that long. He thought for a moment and with a little chuckle he said, "There are two people in this world that I would trust with my very life." He took his weathered hand and with a stretched out finger pointed it at the picture of Jesus hanging above their family piano and said, "He is one." Then he took that same finger and pointed it at his wife and said "she is the other, and that's the way it should be. Never in our 65 years of marriage have I ever doubted that fact." At the moment he pointed his finger in his wife's direction, it was like the clock had been turned back 65 years, because the smile she sent back his way made her look like a 25 year old adoring bride on her wedding day. With a quiet, humble and tearful reply, she looked back at him and said "me too." After an emotional prayer, I left that house praying to Jesus that I would become the kind of man that allowed my wife to say that she never doubted me a single day in our marriage.

Two and a half weeks later, she sat by his bedside. His body had turned weak and frail and about three days later, he finally fell asleep in Jesus. While he still had the strength to speak, he looked her in the eye and said, "I'll see you in the morning," just like he had every night for 65 years. She knew exactly what he meant, and to this day she remembers the look in his eye and holds on to those words.

The person you marry should be the kind of person you would trust in a foxhole; in the heat of battle and when your life is on the line. Jesus never designed people to complete us; only He can do that. This world is a battlefield. There are snares and disasters around every corner. There is heartache and death, disease, and poverty. The list could cover hundreds of pages. We spent much of the last chapter discussing what the brain does when it's "lovesick," and how in our culture we've associated love with these chemical reactions in the brain. However, there is another kind of love that leaves psychologists and Darwinists stumped. It defies all evolutionary logic, and it's called "companionate love"[41]. . This is the kind of love that is not founded on love sickness, but has moved well beyond those fleeting passions. Sexuality is just a piece of companionate love. Selfish gain has no place in companionate love, where each spouse lives for the wellbeing of the other. The only explanation is that it is supernatural. This is the kind of intimacy that we are longing for. This is the kind of intimacy we are trying to create but never will, even by editing our identity in social media. This is the kind of relationship that cannot be found, but can only be made over years of learning the selflessness of God. Communication, desire, service, care, and empathy are all the foundations for a life-long love and the work of the transformative power of the ministry of Jesus in heaven, and the Holy Spirit in our hearts.

Companionate love is shared between two people who have common interests. Trying to be something we are not would totally destroy the possibility of experiencing it. Companionate love exists between two people who live to fulfill the godly dreams of their spouse; their lives are in sync. Companionate love lays down the interests of self, so that the other can grow. Companionate love has the kind of intimacy that can only be truly experienced by people who know the heart of Christ's unselfishness. Companionate love is totally invested in the life of the beloved. When the storms of life come, it stands strong. When things are peaceful, it grows.

God is our constant companion. As we invite Him to a close relationship with us we become transformed to His image. As we become like Him, we really learn to love. When we learn to love like this we can love a spouse as they deserve, and as God intended. We were never intended to complete another person, but as we become like Jesus, we can be a perfect compliment for someone else; so much so that they would trust us with their very life. I pray that God makes me that kind of man. He is my constant companion, therefore, I can be a constant companion to my wife—her compliment and helper.

> "This is My commandment, that you love one another as I have loved you." —John 15:12

If you believe that relationships, love and sexuality will make you happy, it never will. If you believe that relationships, love and sexuality can make you more holy, you will always be happy.

---

41   Ashford, J. B.; et al. (2009). *Human Behavior in the Social Environment*. Gardners Books. p. 498.

Chapter 14
Hookups Are Breaking God's Heart

An increasing amount of single people are turning to arranged marriage to find a spouse. Before you close this book because you think I'm crazy, think through this for a moment. In an arranged marriage a parent—or matchmaker in some cultures—takes into consideration certain details about a person: age, health, family, goals, morals, religion, income, upbringing, where a person lives, future potential, ability to raise a family etc. Based on these details, a man and woman are matched. The interesting thing about arranged marriages is that they typically last. One factor contributing to this statistic is that in many of the countries where this is practiced, divorce is often viewed as a taboo. Another factor is that for many of these cultures, particularly in Asia, marriage doesn't have the westernized belief about "love." It's about how the newly married couple can help their families and contribute to society. These couples understand that love is not something to be experienced totally before the wedding day, but is to be developed over a lifetime together. After many years of marriage, these same couples report that they stayed together because of love. It is a common myth that arranged marriages are loveless marriages, when in fact, many couples report a great love and respect for one another.

A recent BBC study on couples who had been together for more than twenty five years, reported that consensus, social support, and economic stability were the three most important factors for happy and stable marriages[42]. It seems that the foundations for stable marriages are much different than the fairy tales fed to us by Hollywood.

A growing number of young adults realize this dynamic. In fact, one single guy I was talking to recently, told me it would just be easier if his parents would arrange a marriage for him. "On the other hand," he said,

---

42   Vernon, Mark. "Down With Romantic Love." *News Magazine*. BBC, 12 02 2013. Web. 19 Oct. 2013. <http://www.bbc.co.uk/news/magazine-21410275>.

"I'm not ready to let this happen because I don't trust my parents to make a good decision." He was half joking, and totally believes in the arranged marriage theory and feels that in a perfect environment it could really work.

If I told you that 54 million people in the United States were totally open to the idea of arranged marriage would you believe me? What if I told you that 54 million people actually are currently accepting that kind of arrangement? It is an absolute fact, and the number is growing every day[43]. Many dating websites and agencies are actually based on the same principles as arranged marriage. When a person joins a dating site they put personal information into a database and then fill out a profile. Next, they answer detailed questions about desired qualities in a potential mate; things like occupation, physical characteristics, family, upbringing, geographic location, health, lifestyle, future potential, socioeconomic status, skills and beliefs concerning children, marriage, and religion. In some cultures people trust their families to make a good decision about arranging a marriage. In the U.S. people trust a computer program, but the methods are fundamentally the same. There are 54 million people in this country currently using dating websites.

Healthy marriages are based on the very things that these arranged relationships are founded on. Making level headed decisions about these all important characteristics can make or break a marriage. Historically, and in societies all over the world, arranged marriages really work. On the other hand, I am not an advocate for dating website relationships. One of the reasons I do not endorse this idea is the same reason that we discussed in the previous chapter. People are so desperate to be loved that they frequently edit their profiles too much. It is too difficult and risky to try and decide who is telling the truth and who isn't. Typically, when someone joins a dating website they are far too focused on *getting in a relationship.* This mindset sets people up for failure, sin, and emotional baggage. I personally have worked with numerous people who have experienced absolute heartache as a result of meeting someone online. It has worked for some, but in my opinion, the risks outweigh the benefits far too much to recommend it. Folks that I have worked with have experienced identity theft, fraud, people pretending to be someone they are not, married people posing as singles, and people looking for relationships only because they need money, among other less grievous issues. We seem to be so mixed up about how to find the right spouse.

---

43   http://www.statisticbrain.com/online-dating-statistics/ Reuters, 6/18/2013

On the complete other end of the spectrum are those who live the hookup culture. Alarmingly, more people than ever are willing to have sex with lovers on a very casual basis, as if sex has no price tag without any regard to marriage at all. Caring less about their future and marriage, they are just living to have "fun." Nightclubs and popular music are filled with the pornographic images of casual sex. Take the lyrics from one recent "clubbing" anthem,

> "There's a stranger in my bed. There's a pounding in my head. Glitter all over the room. Pink flamingos in the pool. I smell like a minibar. DJ's passed out in the yard. Barbies on the barbecue. Is this a hickey or a bruise?" —*Last Friday Night (T.G.I.F.)* Katy Perry. [44]

A recent study revealed something especially troubling— "both men and women had nearly double the amount of hookups as first dates." [45]

The hookup culture has been promoted in popular culture, media, and movies. It has now become an accepted part of college life. One young man who had just returned home from a Seventh-day Adventist college spoke with me about the condition of the school itself. He told me that he was expecting something different, but his friends were frequent porn users. He had been personally asked to be involved in a homosexual relationship and sexual activity seemed much more frequent among students than he ever would have expected. In colleges as a whole (Christian and secular) the statistics are staggering, The most recent data suggest that between 60% and 80% of North American college students have had some sort of hookup experience. [46]

This is not just a problem in colleges, "Similarly, in a sample of seventh, ninth, and 11th graders, 32% of participants had experienced sexual intercourse and 61% of sexually experienced teenagers reported a sexual encounter outside the context of a dating relationship; this represents approximately one fifth of the entire sample." [47]

---

44 Katy Perry *Last Friday Night*. Album: Teenage Dream, 2012 Capital Records.

45 Reid, Julie. "Casual Hookups to Formal Dates." *Gender and Society*. 27.5 (2013): 5. Web. 3 Oct. 2013.

46 Garcia, Jutin. "Sexual Hookup Culture: A Review." *General Psychology Review*. 16.2 (2012): 161–176. Print.

47 Manning WS, Giordano PC, Longmore MA. Hooking up: The relationship contexts of "non-relationship" sex. Journal of Adolescent Research. 2006; 21:459–483.

Living in the last days, we all expected this, but I imagine it is far worse right now than many of us thought. The days of Noah are really here.

"But as the days of Noah were, so also will the coming of the Son of Man be." —Matthew 24:37

In the Days of Noah

"Then the LORD saw that the wickedness of man was great in the earth, and that every intent of the thoughts of his heart was only evil continually." —Genesis 6:5

The most disturbing part about all of this is that young adults are convinced that this is simply a normal part of life. They have come to accept that it is a part of growing up. In fact, in remembering some of my college teammates, this lifestyle was almost like a rite of passage into adulthood. A lot of the guys believed it was their personal right to live an absolutely insane lifestyle while they still could and before they had to "grow up." Many of them actually talked about getting married and having a great wife and kids later in life, but wanted to live this lifestyle before they settled down. It is absolutely vital that the church teaches its youth the advantages of biblical courtship, and single-hood.

A disturbing trend among the leaders and parents of the church is that we are still encouraging dating. I have discovered that many church leaders and parents do not know that over the last ten to fifteen years, the landscape of dating has vastly changed in our culture. What dating meant to my parents is something much different than what it means today. Many in my parent's generation think of dating as two people casually getting to know each other to consider marriage. Dating today is something much different. For teens and young adults, the word "date" has automatic sexual overtones involved. Many people in secular culture especially, believe that the third date is the sex date. It is actually referred to this way. There is a progressive level of physical and emotional intimacy involved with each date in order for it to be successful. Often these relationships are compared less by the qualities of a person and the level of emotional intimacy, than they are by the progression through physical sexuality.

Even in the church, there are an overwhelming amount of parents who have totally submitted to this reality, telling their kids to date, but 'use protection' if sex happens. A growing number of parents feel they cannot prevent relationships, thus willingly foster long-term romantic relationships between their teens and a significant other. Many of these parents think dating is inevitable and they must just allow it to happen because 'kids will be kids'. For some reason we have just accepted the idea that 'dating' is a normal and integral part of life. It presented enough challenges in past generations when it wasn't *as* sexually charged (it always has been to some degree), but now, in the 21st century, it is every bit more dangerous than ever.

George and the Ice Cream Truck

George is overweight and wants to get in shape. He has been to health programs at his church. He has great parents encouraging him, and friends to help him. One day George meets Polly who drives an ice cream truck. She goes all over the community selling treats to children. The greatest part of the job, as everyone knows, is that ice cream truck drivers get all the ice cream they can eat. In fact, it's encouraged as part of the 'ice cream truck culture'. George and Polly strike up a friendship. George's parents encourage him to spend time with Polly as she goes around town selling ice cream. They think it will help him develop good business skills. George wants to lose weight, but just can't seem to control his appetite. You tell me how much weight George will lose over that summer.

For some reason we have accepted that dating, and even having exclusive relationships during early youth are a positive arrangement, in order to learn how to relate to the opposite sex. Somewhere along the line in our thinking, a date became a great place to get to know someone. In fact, a date is a terrible place to get to know someone. Even in the most innocent of situations, attraction, brain chemistry, excitement, peer pressure, are overwhelming forces that can seriously cloud decision-making abilities. Everyone knows that people are on their best behavior around someone they have feelings for anyway, so the person you are dating is actually not projecting their true relaxed self or true character in the first place. It often takes many dates and a lot of time alone to break down those feelings of insecurity; and by this time many have already made a sexual mistake in that relationship. It's interesting how we have been convinced that we can have a sexual relationship without really revealing our true self.

How is a date or an exclusive relationship much different than our situation with George and Polly? Ice Cream is good. It's part of Polly's culture to eat it. George is around it with every encouragement to eat it. He has heard lots of great information about healthy living, but is surrounded by the very temptation he's trying to avoid in a culture that totally promotes 'ice cream eating'. How much harder could it be to make a good decision?

There are schools I have personally visited that are on totally opposite ends of the spectrum when it comes to handling the guy/girl dynamic. One school I visited, kept the guys and girls completely separated and communication between the sexes was forbidden. This approach, in my opinion, is counter-productive because it doesn't teach appropriate biblical friendships between men and women. Denying this extremely important education can make for mistakes and discomfort later in life.

On the other hand, other schools promote pairing up to go to dinners and prom-like events. This is a very risky venture. The moment you pair up boys and girls, sexual tension and pressure automatically follow. I was following one Facebook feed about one such event. It began with a photo of a guy and girl attending a banquet together. The first five comments on that photo were by friends from the same academy about the two dating and getting romantically involved. The comment back from the person who posted the photo was "Oh, it's just a banquet." Really? It didn't seem that way to the other students from the same school. This past year, a number of Christian academies contacted me for help with managing situations where guys and girls were caught having sexual relations on campus. To me, social events like these, and allowing boys and girls to relate at this level on academy campuses is too risky and sends the wrong message to teens. The risks outweigh the benefits. I have personally been approached by middle-aged men and women with tears in their eyes who shared with me stories about the emotional pain that events like this caused them. They still remember it to this day. It had an effect on how they related to the opposite sex later in life. Friendship feasts can be held without the 'dating' innuendos or pairing of boys and girls at all.

God's Plan for Falling in Love

So, is there a way to possibly apply the principles of arranged marriage that 54 million people are paying money to internet sites to use, without actually joining a dating site? Within our culture, how do we achieve the success of the arranged marriage culture even though we don't live in a culture where it's accepted or desired? How do we teach healthy courtship, and its proper timing within the life of an individual? Can you really get to know someone outside of a date?

In a previous chapter, we discussed God's purpose for marriage. God desires a 'oneness' with us. This is understood and exemplified through the relationship of a godly man and wife. It's no wonder that the hookup culture and dating landscape have taken hold. If Satan can affect your future marriage through numerous sexual experiences before the fact, he has had a large influence on your union before you even meet your future spouse. If single-hood and marriage is so important to God, it stands to reason that He would give us some kind of structure for falling in love; a plan we can practically implement based on what He deems best. Said differently, if marriage is God's plan, God would then give us an example of biblical courtship. The question is where do we find it?

God has been madly in love with mankind since before we were created. There have been times in our history that we have forgotten Him. One of the most difficult and heart breaking stories in the history between God and His people took place in the land of Egypt. The descendants of Jacob had come to live in Egypt after Joseph, one of his sons, had become a ruler of Egypt. For many years the Israelites lived in Egypt in peace and worshipped their God in fullness of heart with the blessing of the Egyptians. Over time the Egyptians forgot Joseph's service, and began to oppress and enslave the Israelites. Because of the oppression and slavery many Israelites forgot their faith and love for the one true God. This bondage lasted four hundred years. Israel had, in past generations, found its very identity in God, now there were only a handful of elders that held on to their faith and traditions. So God sent a man named Moses who would lead Israel out of bondage and into the Promised Land, that they could worship God and have a relationship with Him. God wanted to re-establish his marriage with Israel.

There was just one problem. Israel couldn't accept God's proposal because they didn't really know who He was.

So God reintroduces Himself.

> "Then Moses said to God, "Indeed, *when* I come to the children of Israel and say to them, 'The God of your fathers has sent me to you,' and they say to me, 'What *is* His name?' what shall I say to them?" And God said to Moses, "I AM WHO I AM." And He said, "Thus you shall say to the children of Israel, 'I AM has sent me to you.'" Moreover God said to Moses, "Thus you shall say to the children of Israel: 'The LORD God of your fathers, the God of Abraham, the God of Isaac, and the God of Jacob, has sent me to you. This *is* My name forever, and this *is* My memorial to all generations.'" —Exodus 3:13–15

The name God instructs Moses to give to Israel has vast and rich meaning, but was given primarily as a reintroduction. He could have given them any one of His other names from the past, but God here tells his people that his name is the pre-existent, transcendent One. And the name itself is an invitation—'get to know me, and my character'. God showed Israel who He was one miracle after another to deliver them from Egypt. God wanted them to know that His name is based on His character, and His character is understood by what they would witness.

He shows them His power as He commands the plagues to fall on Egypt. God does miraculous things that reveal His character— starting especially with the last plague.

I Am—the Passover lamb,

> "I will sacrifice myself for you, my blood will deliver you from the curse of death."

> "… Behold! the Lamb of God who takes away the sin of the world!" —John 1:29

> "For I will pass through the land of Egypt on that night, and will strike all the firstborn in the land of Egypt, both man and beast; and against all the gods of Egypt I will execute judgment: I *am* the LORD. Now the blood shall be a sign for you on the houses where you *are.* And when I see the blood, I will pass over you; and the plague shall not be on you to destroy *you* when I strike the land of Egypt." —Exodus 12:12, 13 (emphasis supplied)

Pharaoh finally agrees to free the slaves that they might follow their God; but this is not where the courtship process stops. God is preparing to ask for a relationship with Israel and leads them on a journey that will reveal His true character and heart to His people.

> "I AM—Your protection."

> "And the LORD went before them by day in a pillar of cloud to lead the way, and by night in a pillar of fire to give them light, so as to go by day and night. He did not take away the pillar of cloud by day or the pillar of fire by night *from* before the people." —Exodus 13:21, 22 (emphasis supplied)

He leads them to the Red Sea and says, "I AM—Your Savior,"

> "And Moses said to the people, 'Do not be afraid. Stand still, and see the salvation of the LORD, which He will accomplish for you today. For the Egyptians whom you see today, you shall see again no more forever.'" —Exodus 14:13.

Israel sees the approaching Egyptian army and feels trapped. So God says, "I AM—your deliverer,"

> "Then the Egyptians shall know that I *am* the LORD, when I have gained honor for Myself over Pharaoh, his chariots, and his horsemen." … Then Moses stretched out his hand over the sea; and the LORD caused the sea to go *back* by a strong east wind all that night, and made the sea into dry *land,* and the waters were divided. So the children of Israel went into the midst of the sea on the dry *ground,* and the waters *were* a wall to them on their right hand and on their left." —Exodus 14:18–22 (emphasis supplied)

A few days after passing through the Red Sea, the people are desperately thirsty and God Says "I AM—your water of life, your Healer,"

> "And the people complained against Moses, saying, "What shall we drink?" So he cried out to the LORD, and the LORD showed him a tree. When he cast *it* into the waters, the waters were made sweet." There He made a statute and an ordinance for them, and there He tested them, and said, "If you diligently heed the voice of the LORD your God and do what is right in His sight, give ear to His commandments and keep all His statutes, I will put none of the diseases on you which I have brought on the Egyptians. For I *am* the LORD who heals you." —Exodus 15:24–26 (emphasis supplied)

The people are totally dependent upon God for food and He says, "I AM—your Bread of Life,"

> "Then the LORD said to Moses, 'Behold, I will rain bread from heaven for you. And the people shall go out and gather a certain quota every day, that I may test them, whether they will walk in My law or not. And it shall be on the sixth day that they shall prepare what they bring in, and it shall be twice as much as they gather daily.'" —Exodus 16:4, 5

> "I AM—your Provider,"

> "And the LORD spoke to Moses, saying, 'I have heard the complaints of the children of Israel. Speak to them, saying, "At twilight you shall eat meat, and in the morning you shall be filled with bread. And you shall know that I *am* the LORD your God."'" —Exodus 16:11, 12 (emphasis supplied)

Their lives are threatened and God says, "I AM—your Warrior, I will fight for you"

"And Moses built an altar and called its name, The-LORD-Is-My-Banner; for he said, 'Because the LORD has sworn: the LORD *will have* war with Amalek from generation to generation.'"
—Exodus 17:15, 16

The Proposal

God has done all of these amazing things to reveal and make Himself known to His people. He was preparing to lead them into the Promised Land so that they may be one with Him forever. After showing them all of these things, God made a marriage proposal to Israel, to prepare them to enter the home he had created for them. As a groom, getting down on one knee, He says this to the people through Moses, You have seen who I AM; will you marry me?

> "You have seen what I did to the Egyptians, and *how* I bore you on eagles' wings and brought you to Myself. Now therefore, if you will indeed obey My voice and keep My covenant, then you shall be a special treasure to Me above all people; for all the earth *is* Mine. And you shall be to Me a kingdom of priests and a holy nation.'" —Exodus 19:4–6 (emphasis supplied)

Please let me translate that for you into a modern day sounding marriage proposal. "You have seen all that I have done for you. I delivered you. I have brought you to freedom, and shown my love for you. You have seen all that I am. If you will accept this proposal, and enter into the marriage covenant with me, you will forever be a special people to me. You will have a place of honor as my bride forever. I will cherish you and honor you. Will you marry me?"

The people responded with an emphatic 'yes' and God instructed them all to prepare themselves for an honored and blessed occasion. He is about to present His wedding vows to them.

I AM the Groom, You Are the Bride. Get Ready!

> "Then the Lord said to Moses, 'Go to the people and consecrate them today and tomorrow, and let them wash their clothes. And let them be ready for the third day. For on the third day the Lord will come down upon Mount Sinai in the sight of all the people.'"
> —Exodus 19:10, 11

He then instructs the people not to do a specific thing; and by abstaining from it He revealed an extremely important truth to Israel. He tells husbands and wives that they should not come near to one another (vs. 15).

Why would God do that? The answer is that this momentous occasion was about every *single* heart accepting the proposal of the *personal* I AM. He is a personal God, who loves marriages and created them, but wanted the people to understand that the true marriage, the one *theirs was,* was a symbol of the marriage between God and each individual person as they trust and obey Him. He did not want husbands and wives together where one might come on behalf of another. On this wedding day, God wanted a personal "I Do" as He gave them His vows.

The church was made ready, the arrangements were made and the bride was prepared. The Groom was standing at the altar looking his beloved bride in the eyes and He uttered His vows.

I AM—My Vows.

"I God, take you, Israel."

"I *am* the LORD your God, who brought you out of the land of Egypt, out of the house of bondage. —Exodus 20:2

"I promise to be your personal God. I will put you first." "You shall have no other gods before Me." Exodus 20:3

"You will be my primary focus, the very center of my life. I will make you my most honored treasure. My focus will always be on you."

"You shall not make for yourself a carved image—any likeness *of anything* that *is* in heaven above, or that *is* in the earth beneath, or that *is* in the water under the earth; you shall not bow down to them nor serve them. —Exodus 20:4, 5

"I AM what my name reveals. I will honor our relationship. You, this day, take the honor of my name with you, and I adore you. Today you change your name. You are my people, I AM your God."

"You shall not take the name of the LORD your God in vain, for the LORD will not hold *him* guiltless who takes His name in vain. —Exodus 20:7

"I AM your rest and peace. In me you find salvation and hope. I AM your Creator. I AM your redeemer. To show this is true I have ordained a weekly celebration for us to commemorate my love for you."

"Remember the Sabbath day, to keep it holy. Six days you shall labor and do all your work, but the seventh day *is* the Sabbath of the LORD your God. *In it* you shall do no work:… For *in* six days the LORD made the heavens and the earth, the sea, and all that *is* in them, and rested the seventh day. Therefore the LORD blessed the Sabbath day and hallowed it." —Exodus 20:8–10

"I AM the One who gives you life, I AM your comforter, I AM your nurturer. I give you earthly families that you may remember me, and know me better." "Honor your father and your mother, that your days may be long upon the land which the LORD your God is giving you." —Exodus 20:12

"I AM your life Giver." "You shall not murder." —Exodus 20:13

"I AM your One true love—To you I AM eternally faithful." "You shall not commit adultery." —Exodus 20:14

"I Am your Provider—I AM Jehovah Jireh."

"You shall not steal." —Exodus 20: 15

"I AM your way, your *TRUTH*, and your life."

"You shall not bear false witness against your neighbor." —Exodus 20:16

"I AM, and always will be your peace and true contentment."

"You shall not covet your neighbor's house; you shall not covet your neighbor's wife, nor his male servant, nor his female servant, nor his ox, nor his donkey, nor anything that *is* your neighbor's." —Exodus 20:17

What a beautiful and magnificent revelation of the character of God. His wedding vows are based on what He has already done for Israel. By reminding them of what He has done for them in the past, He invites them to love Him, and submit themselves to their relationship with Him. Even the Ten Commandments themselves are a revelation of the name "I AM." Within these vows is a promise that God will continue to be what He has already been for His bride, but also in their obedience to these laws, Israel would continue to experience the happiness and realize the perfect order that comes from mankind joining their hearts with the Author of life.

"If you love me, keep my commandments." —John 14:15.

God Left Standing at the Altar

Imagine the horror of the Groom standing at the altar, communicating his vows through Moses, while His bride, the children of Israel have an orgy around a golden calf idol. Israel left God standing at the altar. The marriage vows had been broken before the marriage license was even signed. For this reason Moses did the following,

> "So it was, as soon as he came near the camp, that he saw the calf *and* the dancing. So Moses' anger became hot, and he cast the tablets out of his hands and broke them at the foot of the mountain" —Exodus 32:19 (emphasis supplied)

Vows Broken

God Heartbroken.

I'm Just Not That In To You

The love of God shines through even though Israel put Him through such pain. He still takes them to the promised land, Canaan, as He promised; the very home that He had prepared for them. A good groom has a home prepared for His bride before they get married. Standing at the outskirts of this home, they send their lookouts into Canaan and view the vast riches and blessings of that land. All but two spies return to report that the enemies in the land are too great; essentially saying that the enemies are bigger and more powerful than God.

Many people look at the judgment of God, for Israel to walk the wilderness for forty years as a harsh judgment. In actuality, it was simply part of the courtship. God used this time as an opportunity to prove Himself worthy of the love of Israel. In the wilderness, God gave Israel one of the greatest gifts ever given to man—the sanctuary service, a visual representation of the love of God, and a picture of His Son because through this Son, the marriage vows would be renewed.

The Marriage Covenant Renewed

Everywhere Israel failed, Jesus was victorious. After forty years in the wilderness Israel still did not fully grasp and accept the love of the Father. Jesus after forty days fasting in the wilderness relied only on the word and character of the Father in His starved, tempted, weak condition. Jesus Himself is the covenant. Through His victory over temptation in the wilderness, His sinless life, His sacrifice, His love for the Father, the submission of His will, His death and laying in the tomb, His resurrection, the Great Commission, and His ministry in Heaven for us, Christ achieved what sinful man could not. Jesus Christ's ministry and the power of the Godhead is what bonds man to Himself forever, if… we decide to love Him, and in this love say 'yes' to the vows by His power.

God as a Suitor

God never asked for the hand of Israel until they knew Him. God even sent His Son so that we may know Him without a doubt. God's model for biblical courtship is the only model that will provide true success. Because of the pressures of the dating culture, and our love-drug dependent brains, the dating scene is far too risky and has become too tainted. You cannot fully know someone by 'dating'. We must train our youth to discern the character of someone, the way God demonstrated His character to Israel, long before there is any hint of romance added to a relationship.

I always tell the young ladies in my seminars not to marry a guy who only opens the door for them, but to marry the guy who opens the door for his mother, and even strangers. Too often people settle for the person they see on a date. It's what we've been trained to do. The only safe and healthy way to know the character of a person is to observe their character without sexual tension, and outside of a relationship. Instead, parents are encouraging their youth to do the opposite—to give their heart and *then* get to know someone. God never asks for our hearts *until* we know Him.

It's All About Timing

Young adults have no business being in relationships until they are in a place in life where they can maturely and fully survey the character of a person, and obey boundaries in courtship. Relationships should only be considered when adding a person in your life would actually help you achieve God's purpose for your life and not hinder it. The younger a person is and the less prepared they are, the more emotional, practical, spiritual, and physical baggage they will carry into their marriage; even if they are one of the very few that marries their high school sweetheart.

How does this work? At every age, girls and guys should be taught to properly be friends with one another—even close friends. But every friendship should have clear boundaries. We need to realize that there are vulnerable situations. It amazes me how many parents will allow two teens or young adults, male and female, to be alone together on their watch. Even teens admit that you can actually get to know someone better as friends around other friends. Where they need the most help from leaders is to know what to do with an attraction or interest in someone;

how to conduct themselves in a Godly and practical way. Friends can and should be viewed as future potential *prospects*, but just because a person is a prospect does not mean we need to give them our heart. It is also vital that we teach them how to observe the true character of a person, and how to identify positive and negative traits. We have to educate our youth that true love is about character, and you cannot know someone's character after a few weeks or even months. I always tell youth to get to know each other really well but not cross the boundary into a relationship. If you enter the point of no return, you automatically add sexual pressure, memories, and baggage. If you want to avoid baggage you had better know the character of a person enough to spend your life with them, and you had better be in a place in life where you are ready to say 'I do'. At the right time for a relationship that person will be there, and if not, there is someone else better suited for them out there, somewhere. In fact, being in an exclusive relationship with someone could actually hinder you from going places and meeting people who could have changed your life in a powerful and providential way.

God never asked for Israel to love Him until after He had proved His character to them. Under this model, courtships should be relatively short, because the pair should already know each other. They should have avoided the many vulnerable hours alone together. In a courtship, there needs to be some alone time to talk, but this must also be done wisely, perhaps in a public place.

Lastly we as leaders need to communicate the privilege that Godly friendship and courtship is. The way we conduct our friendships or courtship reveals our love for God. How we submit our love lives to Him will reveal the degree of God's influence we desire in our marriages. If God is love, there is so much more to romance than the current dating and hook-up culture. If He is true love, then the marriages that follow His plan for courtship would be the most incredible institutions on the planet. We are not depriving ourselves by doing things God's way. We are gaining a marriage that has supernatural potential. We are following a plan that is set out by the true Author of Love.

The Biblical Courtship Model—In a Perfect World.

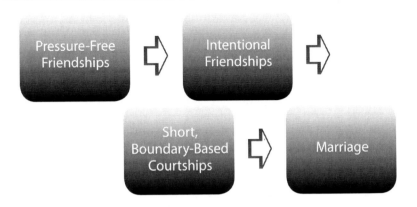

Pressure Free Friendships—In this step, teens, younger college students, and people unsure of their future are to make friends without the pressure of expecting to be in a romantic relationship. This allows a person to freely take mental notes about people, and learn how to positively interact with people of the opposite sex. Close friends from this stage might be potential prospects later.

Intentional Friendships—This stage is a narrowing down of the friendship circle. It means intentionally spending time with a person or persons who share your common interests, goals, and values. In seeking a mate, it is important to ask a person specifically to spend time with you among friends to get to know each other better. Setting up these circumstances and events is very important, but should be conducted without the pressure of a date, or a relationship. People often fear entering the "friend zone," because it could hinder any romance later. It's interesting, however, the number of people who report that their spouse is their best friend. If you are going to consider marrying someone, why consider a stranger? Why not a close friend? Intentionally developing a progression in a friendship allows for people to create intimacy without sexual pressure. This portion of the model helps a person avoid multiple romances, and courtships. If you are intentional about friendships you already know a marital prospect before you begin a courtship with them. Essentially, a courtship is a possible engagement. Because of this, it is necessary for these "intentional friends" to spend some time together—the two of them. To maintain friendship status, it is important to apply strict boundaries. They should arrive and depart from places separately and should always be in public.

The "intentional friends" step is especially vital for young professionals who are no longer in college, or have a large friendship base to draw from and rely on. People must be taught how to develop healthy friendships that are intentional without the relationship pressure.

Courtship—After getting to know a person intimately as a friend, this stage allows for a couple to spend time together to discuss and consider marriage in the near future under the protection of boundaries and accountability. Please note, a long relationship is not necessarily courtship. Some people think that because they have been exclusive with someone for a long time that they are courting. Unless there are marriage plans being considered and made, it is not courtship.

Stories of Godly Courtships

They knew each other as kids. She always had her eye on him. In fact the childhood fantasies about marrying him one day actually entered her adult mind on several occasions. They went to the same academy together, and had many of the same friends. They never crossed the romantic line. They ended up going to different colleges, but by chance enrolled in the same summer colporteur program after their junior year of college. This is when things got more serious. Relationships between program participants were discouraged during the summer program but this did not stop them from remembering all their childhood experiences as they met nightly for fellowship. They spent their senior year of school focusing on their grades and called each other frequently. As they graduated, they decided that when they returned home after graduation, they would sit down and seriously discuss their future together (they both told me that their minds had actually been made up long before that summer). In a park that July, they met together. During this meeting they decided it was God's will that they spend the next few months in courtship with the direct intention of pursuing marriage. For the next two months they spent time at each other's homes with family; intentionally staying out of vulnerable situations. He spent time with her parents, she with His. They frequently went to dinner with friends. After about nine weeks, he approached her father to ask for her hand in marriage. They were married six months later. Oh, and might I add that their first kiss was shared after they said "I do."

This is not the only story like this. Just like the other couple that did Bible work together for two years before they even considered each other in a romantic way, when these two finally did, it was an easy and romantic transition into marriage. He now is a full time evangelist who has an adoring wife who understands his work and supports his schedule.

Greg and Angie met in college and simply started to hang out with the same people, getting to know each other. After about seven months of friendship, she was the first to mention to him that they made a great match and were married during spring break of their senior year—never having 'dated'. Getting to know each other by meeting with a group of friends nightly for fellowship and Bible study, even their courtship was chaperoned by friends who wanted to hold them accountable. The last semester of their senior year, they served as a married chaperone couple for another couple from their group of friends who were courting in much the same way.

The good news is that there is a growing movement of young people who will not accept the current status of love, romance, and sexuality. Not every story is exactly the same, but the bottom line is that there is a true God of every true love story. What must take place is for each young and single person to reject the message about how a true romance must take place, even though this idea has been pounded into our heads from the first time we saw a Disney movie. True love is Jesus, and He is the Author of true love for us. In fact, most of the love stories people want their lives patterned after, are fiction. The love story between God and Israel is absolutely true. The love story He wants to write in the life of every person is just as amazing as His work to reveal Himself to Israel so long ago.

Chapter 15
Why We Don't Talk About It

You might be waiting for a very fancy answer to this dilemma, or something very complicated. Yet the answer is far from complicated and strikes deeply within our personal emotions and history. The reason we don't talk about biblical sexuality is because if we do, we would have to do something about it. What do I mean by this? It does no good to talk about a real, challenging issue and not provide help and solutions. As our culture grows increasingly busier and self-centered, it becomes more messy and difficult to invest in the life of someone else. Yet this kind of investment is exactly what it will take to change the sexual culture in our church. To really help someone change we run the risk of that help changing us.

For many of us this is a very uncomfortable venture.

As we have read in this book there is an end-time attack on the character of God and the Gospel itself. Sexuality is not just about marriage, diseases, and personal purity. It is about how we reflect the character of God to the world. It cannot be taken lightly.

More than ever before our kids are getting their sex education from their friends and Google searches. Pornography is easily accessible. More teens than ever are questioning their sexuality. And the church remains silent... And the Sexy Beast is devouring us from within.

The Challenges:

1. If we talk about it, we will be convicted about it. I was talking to a young man and his father one day about dating and sexuality. The young man was a teen, and he had already begun to date numerous girls. His dad had brought him to me so that I could talk to him about it, and hopefully "set him straight." He himself had not known how to address it. After I was finished visiting with the young man, his dad turned to me and said with a smile on his face,

"Well, it's no wonder we are going through this, he's just like his dad—a real ladies man. I had my share of girlfriends and made my share of mistakes."

My mouth was hanging open. If Jesus was not holding me back, I might have slapped this guy across the forehead. I knew immediately why he had a hard time talking to his own son. The reason was that he himself was struggling with sexual impurity. Now he was a happily married man who no doubt was faithful to his wife. The trouble is that if he could look back at his past and still smile about his sexual exploits, he had not really repented of them in his heart. It must be our hearts cry "create in me a clean heart," (Psalm 51). Too many of us have asked for forgiveness for the act, but still love the memories they carry. We need to realize that cherishing the memory of sin is as bad as the sin itself. It is the same impurity revisited.

To research this topic enough and to talk about it with our youth would bring conviction to our own hearts. Any good preacher will tell you that his sermons are as much for him as they are for the church. In telling others, we ourselves are reminded. When we are reminded, we must decide if we want to change. If we change, it might dig up cherished sins from our past. If we change, it might affect our entertainment choices. If we change, we might have to fight our wandering eyes in public and on the internet. Change is uncomfortable, so we would rather not talk about something that is so convicting to us. Is it possible that our reticence to talk about sexuality is because it reveals our lack of consecration? I know in my ministry the sins I am struggling with are the hardest to preach about. God never calls perfect people to preach because He knows that the preaching and teaching themselves will help those that are standing in the pulpit.

Too many of us get pleasure thinking about the sexual sins of our past. I have personally spoken to many fathers who think that they cannot talk to their sons about pornography because they themselves watch it. One of the greatest obstacles for us in taking down the sexy beast is the sexual sins in our own lives. Perhaps some of us have made mistakes in the past and never really repented of them at all. A sin is only an outward act of a greater struggle in our heart, by failing to repent, that part of our character cannot be renewed by Christ. Remember, the problem with purity is that we don't talk about it in a Christ-centered way. There is forgiveness and there is victory. This message can save us and those who we have been called to teach.

"There is great need of the Holy Spirit's influence in our midst. There must be an individual work done in the breaking of stubborn hearts. There needs to be deep heart-searching that will lead to confession of sin. Believers should at this time stand with softened, sanctified, broken hearts, and confess every sin in repentance that needs to be repented of. The Holy Spirit is waiting to kindle in the heart the love of God, that His praise may be spoken from lips that are true, unselfish, clean, and honest. When holy principles guide the life, the soul will be beautiful in its simplicity. ... Every individual is under obligation to give to others the truth he possesses. Nothing should be allowed to keep the servant of Christ from letting his light shine forth to his fellow men. ... We should be daily increasing in ability to do the precious work of winning souls to Christ. This is such a precious work, such a satisfying work!" [48]

Jesus is light and purity. He wants to bring purity to our homes, marriages, and children. Sins we're brushing under the rug or have set away for many years will show up in our lives in other areas and affect our kids.

"For the word of God *is* living and powerful, and sharper than any two-edged sword, piercing even to the division of soul and spirit, and of joints and marrow, and is a discerner of the thoughts and intents of the heart. And there is no creature hidden from His sight, but all things *are* naked and open to the eyes of Him to whom we *must give* account." —Hebrews 4:12, 13 (emphasis supplied)

God knows what is in our hearts. He knows why we aren't talking about biblical sexuality and the real struggles our church is going through. It's time that we allowed Him to purify us by talking about it with others.

This reluctance to talk about it can also come from *pain* in the past. Sexual abuse is not a new thing. There are church leaders and many parents who have been sexually abused and have a hard time talking about sexuality because of that pain. Get help! Find a friend to talk to and a trained and accredited Christian counselor who is Bible based, and supports your faith. It will be vital for you to work through some of those issues with them. If you are not able to talk about sexuality, it is a sign that the pain from your past affects you more greatly than you may have expected.

---

48   White, Ellen. "Our Duty to Communicate Truth." *Adventist Review.* 25 02 1909: n. page. Print.

2. Investing in a life. Time and time again youth and young adults tell me that the greatest desire they have in their Christian walk is for an older person to take an interest in their lives and mentor them. They desperately want to be able to go to someone that they trust with questions and for help. Becoming a mentor certainly calls for us to break out of the old routine. It calls for us to be a family with the church outside the church walls. Being a mentor to someone means investing in their life and loving and caring for them. It calls for listening, correcting in love, guiding, and teaching. At a recent camp meeting I led out a brain storming session with a group of young adults on how they could make a difference in their church. We talked for two hours about how they could become mentors for teens. They never had one growing up and felt like it was the greatest need in the church today. While it was great to hear them share their desire to step up to the plate and be there for youth, it also shows the sad truth that they feel the need to be mentors because there are far too few willing to fill that role.

We are living in the Great Controversy. We have been called to help each other live through it. The youth need the help from elders by word and deed; acts of love. They will sometimes fail, but loving them through failure to victory is what we have been called to do. There are many *warm* and friendly churches, but there are very few *mentoring* churches.

Current Seventh-day Adventist General Conference president Ted Wilson said of this great need,

> "When young adults look for a mentor, they will probably start with their parents. But then they will look to people who really seem to be trustworthy, not people who are just trying to show off or be a big name, but people who they sense are genuine, humble Christians from whom they could learn something. When they approach that someone, they will want to be listened to and share, not receive a lecture. One of the most important things about dealing with young adults is to have open communication, always be willing to talk, always be willing to share, and always be ready to listen." [49]

While I agree with Elder Wilson, I would take his statement a step further. I would suggest that people should not wait until the youth approach them, but should actively seek out the youth. It's great to have parents as mentors, but those youth who don't have those strong role models and

---

49   http://www.adventistworld.org/article/972/resources/english/issue-2011-1004/young-ready

are unlikely to seek out a mentor themselves, need people to step up to the responsibility. Of all the solutions in this book that are vital to combat the false sexual gospel, following the Great Commission is the most powerful one. Within the Great Commission is a call to be a mentor.

"Go therefore and make disciples of all the nations, baptizing them in the name of the Father and of the Son and of the Holy Spirit." —Matthew 28: 19

Preaching is only the beginning. *To make a disciple, is to invest in a life.* As a pastor I have seen churches transformed when they train each other and mentor the youth to win souls for Jesus. As a youth leader I have seen the lives of young adults changed when they are mentored to lead people to Jesus-making disciples.

I knew a young man I will call Jim. Jim's family brought him up in the faith, but when he became a teen, he got into drugs and alcohol and seldom came to church. One day a group of young adults, who were planning a mission trip, invited Jim to come with them to reach that community. At first he said no, but the invitations were so frequent and convincing that he finally accepted. So here was Jim, a druggie himself, going through this community trying to reach people for Jesus. Through this experience Jim's heart was converted, and he was re-baptized on the mission trip along with people he was reaching himself. He never did drugs or drank alcohol again, and now Jim is a big part of the youth group that invited him to go on the mission trip. Jim's conversion was part of a great mentoring story. Jim was mentored by other youth. This is the best formula for success. These youth had been mentored by elders in their churches. Mentoring creates an environment for trust, love, appreciation, and conversion. Just ask Jim.

Jesus says, "A disciple is not above his teacher, but everyone who is perfectly trained will be like his teacher" (Luke 6:40). We are learning everyday. Who is teaching us and guiding us makes all the difference.

How a Mentor Saved Me

In my personal life, I have experienced the power of a church leader investing in me, and mentoring me, and it made all the difference. I was a fourth-generation member of the church. I sat in kindergarten, primary, juniors, early teen, teen, and youth Bible class. I sat, listened, and learned. I also sat in baptismal class, marked my paper "yes" to be baptized, and was baptized. But somewhere along the way, the information, songs, stories, and baptism didn't translate into an understanding of who God wanted me to be, or who I thought I was supposed to be.

Had my pastors failed? Not really, they did the best they knew. Did my church fail? Certainly not, for they did as much as they knew to do.

I didn't want to attend a Christian college because I had other interests, never understanding church school or the need for it. So, I sat in class, in lab, listened to the information, and somehow the information didn't really translate into an understanding of who God wanted me to be. I even had a powerful experience with Jesus on a pitching mound one day. After that point, God used me as a witness, but still the world around me came crashing in. I had so many questions.

I longed for a friend, but because many of my friends were into alcohol and partying, I didn't spend much time with them. I knew what was right in God's eyes, and was struggling to live it. I longed for a call from someone in my church—a peer. No calls came. My belief in the truth of the church remained, but my faith was very small. I always knew Christ was there and I loved Him, so that saved me from some bad decisions, but because I didn't have anyone around me to help sort through life, I didn't make *all* the right decisions.

I had very good parents. They did their very best; loved me, cared for me, taught me well, but somehow their love didn't translate into an understanding of who God wanted me to be. They modeled faith, but it never became personal.

My last two years of college, I spent questioning. I was constantly testing how near the line of worldly living I could get without totally crossing it; while still trying to share my faith. It was odd. I was known to others as a firm believer and put on a good show; witnessed to many people. But deep down, I was struggling. There were things I rationalized as ok, that clearly were not. But in my heart there was a pain, a dull ever-present pain that made me unsatisfied and discontent. I was trying to feast on the dry husks of the world around me. I didn't know how to take the Jesus that lived in my heart and translate that faith into a practical life outside of my heart. I knew my faith in my mind, but it was more a collection of 'true things' to me than an actual living truth. I believe this is a huge struggle of many young Christian people.

One day an elder from the church approached me. He asked me to preach. With nervous feelings, and thoughts of hypocrisy on my mind I accepted. As I began to work on my sermon something clicked. A fire began to burn within me, and my hand flew across the page as I wrote with inspiration. My mind was moving quickly with all I remembered from my upbringing and all those Sabbath schools I had sat through. Now that I had been called upon, all of what I learned began to click and it all made sense.

After the sermon was preached, there were many compliments, many words of encouragement, and many praises to God for the message. This young man felt great, but it didn't last. After I went home from church the feelings of purpose began to die away; the fire did not last. It returned one day when I was asked to preach again. The same experience happened. All I knew and loved deep within me clicked again, and soon an inner turmoil began to arise. I still had one year of college left to attend. Now the two sermons I preached battled against the lack of faith I had in my heart. The fine line I was walking in my life began to conflict with the words I was preaching from the front. It would be nice to say that everything changed immediately, but I didn't. The fire died down, the conviction dulled, and I walked ever closer to a dangerous line my entire senior year of college. Upon graduation my college community went away. I felt friendless and confused about my direction. This left me wondering what God wanted for me, or if God even cared. The church began to seem irrelevant and cumbersome because no one really showed much of an interest in me being there.

Then something significant happened. A new pastor came to our district. This new pastor soon began planning an evangelistic crusade series in my local community. This pastor had heard that I was a gifted preacher. Without reservation and without hesitation this pastor sat me down and invited me to co-preach this series of meetings with him.

Deep in my heart, I longed that what I had learned from my childhood, witnessed from my parents, and experienced at times when I was alone with God would return. I knew that this was my opportunity for the fire to come back, for the feelings of purpose and identity to return, and maybe, just maybe, it would last for good. This pastor worked with me, and taught me what it meant to win souls. He taught me how to be a better preacher. His investment in my life made a huge impact on me. I preached in the crusade series and people gave their hearts to Jesus, and so did I. The rest is history.

I wish I could say all the stories of our youth have happy endings like mine. I wish we could look out at our congregations and see people that are 18–35 with young families, a vibrant part of the leadership of our churches. I wish I could say that our churches know exactly how to engage youth and young adults and utilize their gifts, but sadly, this would not be the truth. Don't get me wrong, we love our youth but we are still struggling.

As I travel around the country speaking to thousands of youth every year the tone seems to be the same—the youth are struggling, like I did, to discover what God wants for their lives and where He is leading them. Sadly, while they are struggling, many are creating heartache and baggage in their lives. The overwhelming message I get from these young people is that they do not trust their church, and as a result many have begun to doubt its message. They see people all around them giving up on God at an alarming rate. They see people still seeking the unconditional love God gives from romance, drugs, gangs, or academics.

I have witnessed this time and time again, a great disconnect between what the young adults want and need and what the church thinks they want and need. While the church is arguing about music and worship styles, the youth are discouraged, knowing deep in their heart that all they really want is to be able to trust the leaders and members of their church and to be empowered by them. Youth are looking for a community of people that love them. They are looking for a place where God can use them. Many of them could care less about the style of music, if they feel that they are free to share their struggles and use their gifts. It is no different with adults who are struggling. Their needs and desires are the same.

People do not leave our church because of the music. They leave because they are longing for a sense of identity and are not finding it in the church. Many feel they find it in sex, relationships, education, career, family, the night club, or their non-Christian friends. We are all just trying to figure out where we fit in life. Trying to find the most easily accessible route to feeling true purpose and love.

Easy Targets

To Satan, youth are especially easy targets. During the developmental stages, the brain is more vulnerable to addiction[50]. The effects of drugs and alcohol actually have a longer, lasting effect; and young brains take longer to recover from the effects. The frontal lobe is not fully developed, creating a challenge to proper decision-making, and self-discipline.

---

50   For more on this go to: http://www.livescience.com/17938-teens-prone-addiction-mental-illness.html

Cultural pressure from peers and family can also affect reasoning. At this teen and young adult developmental period is when parents see the greatest changes in the behavior of their kids. Some parents describe their kids as "aliens" or "strangers." Much of this new behavior can be attributed to a developing brain. The frontal lobe of the brain is accessible, but it is not fully connected. Because of raging hormones, a desire for independence, and many other reasons, decisions can be made that will negatively affect a person for a lifetime. Many teens seem love sick, and some of them seem addicted to sexuality. The potent cocktail that is released during sexual contact is addictive. Thus addictive behavior coupled with a developing frontal lobe can create a very vulnerable lifestyle.

Staggering Reality

According to the American Sexual Health Association, each year one out of every four teens contracts a new STD.

About 330,000 babies were born to girls ages 15–19 in 2011. [51]

If a teen is to become sexually active, the most common age is 17; while the most common age for marriage is the mid 20s. [52]

Psychology Today recently published an article that links sexual promiscuity to depression and substance abuse. [53]

According to the *New York Times* 1 in 12 teens have attempted suicide. [54]

These stats are terrifying and hopefully an eye opener. Please notice that these stats were not based on non-Christians. Sometimes we attribute these struggles to youth outside the church. But as I write here, I have tears in my eyes remembering the youth who have come to me and told me about their problems with pornography, cutting (a self-destructive behavior that involves the use of pain to stimulate a desired neurological and physical response), substance abuse, depression, and promiscuity. These are our kids, in our church. Many of them are our leaders. The

51 American Sexual Health Association STD Statistics. http://www.ashasexualhealth.org/std-sti/std-statistics.html

52 Guttmacher Institute. Facts on American Teens' Sexual and Reproductive Health. http://www.guttmacher.org/pubs/FB-ATSRH.html. October 2013.

53 Uche, Ugo. "A Link Between Sexual Promiscuity and Depression in Teens." *Promoting Empathy With Your Teen*. Psychology Today, 14 01 2013. Web. 3 Oct. 2013.

54 Neal, Megan. "1 in 12 Teens Have Attempted Suicide." *New York Times* [New York, NY] 09 06 2012, Weekend n. pag. Print.

question for us is not, 'why are they leaving'? We know why they leave. We have seen it first hand in our own congregations. The question is, 'what can the church do about it?'

Mentoring an Identity

The way to save our youth and our church in the process is actually much easier than we think. It involves our personal God given commission. It involves much more than just a desperate attempt at reclaiming our youth using desperate methods. "Save our church," you might be thinking? Consider this, within 10 years of me writing this in 2013, 50% of all the ministers and leadership in the U.S. will be retired. We are missing our youth in the churches. We are missing the next generation of leaders[55].

You see, the church has an identity crisis. The reason our youth are missing is because of the same struggle I had; an identity crisis. The reason youth have not stepped up as the next generation of leaders is because of an identity crisis. Who are we? Why are we here? In planning for the Second Coming have we forgotten to mentor the next generation? Have we believed that because we were converted to a truth that the same truth will automatically give our youth an identity?

In every young person there are three ideas about identity that they struggle with. 1. Who God has made us to be. 2. Who we think we are. 3. The person our culture tells us we should be. At any one moment any, or all three, may be the face we are trying to put on.

Society tells us that our sexual urges, interests, intelligence, upbringing, socio-economic status, race, athletic ability, determine who we are and the future we will live.

Our faith, church, and our conscience tell us how we should live and to be a certain person.

Our own desires and dreams, our heart tells us how we should live and be a certain person.

At times there is a mixture of all three; sometimes we are just one. We are always looking for affirmation and confirmation in everyday life, faith,

55   Oliver, Ansel. "Implications of Aging Ministers Could Challenge Future Staffing." *Adventist News Network.* 08 05 2012: n. page. Web. 3 Oct. 2013. <http://news.adventist.org/en/archive/articles/2012/05/08/implications-of-aging-ministers-could-challenge-future-staffing>.

opportunities and community; testing the ground to decide which voice about our identity is telling the truth.

What must be discussed next is the most terrifying part. While youth are on this journey to find purpose, Satan loves to pile on baggage. Life altering events, relationships, memories, abuse, teen pregnancies, drug use, depression and anxiety, the list is nearly infinite. As compared to our entire life span, birth through young adulthood is the shortest stretch of life, yet the most life-altering. Events during this time will help shape the rest of our lives.

A Lover or a Role Model?

I was recently talking with a college-age young lady. She came to me in tears after one of my seminars. She said that her parents were always too busy to put her first over their careers. She said she never really learned what a Christian was, even though her parents had brought her up in the church. In order to feel loved and appreciated, she found a young man who would provide what she thought would fill this void in her heart. The relationship escalated, got sexual, and now she felt trapped. She didn't want to leave the relationship because it was the only place she felt love, yet the feeling of guilt for the things she was doing in the relationship were unbearable. As we were talking though, she said she would rather feel the guilt than to feel alone. The next question I asked broke my heart. I asked her "What about your church"? She scowled at me and laughed in a very frustrated way. She had tried to talk to people there but they had either betrayed her confidence, or said something like "well you have to trust Jesus." That was the extent of their interest in her.

The way to save our youth is the same way we save the world; by making disciples. We expose the sexy beast the same way we expose the end time anti-Christ, by preaching the truth. Just as Jesus made disciples we too need to mentor others.

The Great Commission is not just to *preach* but also to *make*. Making disciples is every bit as important as preaching. Something powerful happens when we mentor and coach people in the work of the Lord. Their lives change and so do ours. This has been missing for far too long in many churches. Every person has been called to be a disciple and to make disciples. The Bible tells us to preach and to,

> "... *teach* ... them to obey all things as I have commanded you."
> —Matthew 28:20 (emphasis supplied)

Jesus not only taught with words, He taught with his own example, by creating opportunities for the disciples to use their gifts, with patience, and with investing His personal time with them. This is the model that took a young man like me who was a great witness on the outside, but was struggling in my heart and brought me to where I needed to be. It has happened with many others like me.

Jesus said teach them "all things." It is not hard to understand why the church has problems with sexual purity. We don't talk about it. It's the elephant in the room. If making disciples of our youth is the way to save our youth, we must teach them to obey all things. It is a message that we cannot leave out. We have ignored it too long. Too many of our own people have been devoured by the Sexy Beast. Sexuality has been a taboo for too long and we're way behind in trying to combat the sinfulness of our culture. Sexuality is part of the gospel itself.

True sexuality reveals the true nature of God—selflessness. If the Great Controversy is over the character of God, then sexuality would be part of the Three Angel's Messages of Revelation fourteen. If we are not teaching it and preaching it while making disciples for Christ, we are not preaching the full gospel. We have already suffered the consequences with too many of our own people, young and old.

We are all called to be ministers, not all ordained ministers, but all full-time Gospel preachers. This is the call for all of us,

> "I charge *you* therefore before God and the Lord Jesus Christ, who will judge the living and the dead at His appearing and His kingdom: Preach the word! Be ready in season *and* out of season. Convince, rebuke, exhort, with all longsuffering and teaching. For the time will come when they will not endure sound doctrine, but according to their own desires, *because* they have itching ears, they will heap up for themselves teachers; and they will turn *their* ears away from the truth, and be turned aside to fables. But you be watchful in all things, endure afflictions, do the work of an evangelist, *fulfill your ministry.*" —2 Timothy 4:1–5 (emphasis supplied)

The time has come. We must fulfill our charge. Our hearts cry out for our youth, and because of the sins of our past. We are the divorced, those with sexually transmitted diseases, those that have had our hearts broken, those who have porn addiction, those who have been sexually abused, those who struggle with lust, those who battle with sin every day. We are those who wanted to save sex for marriage but made a mistake, those with relationship baggage that has affected our current marriages, those whose sexual sins have affected our witness for Jesus.

We are those who must be the voices crying out for the truth. We must never allow the sexy beast to devour our children, our youth, or our young leaders. Jesus is coming soon and it is time we allowed Jesus to tell us—like He did the woman at the well—all the things we have ever done; and forgive, cleanse, and empower us through His ministry in Heaven that we may "Go and sin no more." It is time we sounded the trumpet. It is time to take down the sexy beast. It is time that Jesus is lifted up in *every* part of our lives. It is time that His purity and His character are present in all our thoughts every moment. It is time to follow the Lamb wherever He goes. It is time.

So what will you do? Will you let the elephant in the room stay there and grow bigger and bigger until he has pushed everyone out of the church? Will you allow the sexy anti-christ message to gnaw away at our church and our youth while you stand idly by and do nothing about it? The way to expose error is to preach Jesus. Jesus created sex so that mankind would know Him better. Will you preach, and teach the full Gospel? Will you mentor a young person and listen to them as they share their struggles and help them answer life's questions? How you answer will reveal how serious you are about obeying the Gospel commission. God is eternally faithful to us, and works daily to win our hearts. Will you give Him yours? If you want to save our youth, your heart must be surrendered to God first. If you want purity in your life, you must fall in love with the God who loved you before you were ever born. It is our responsibility to make a stand for purity in our lives. It is our responsibility to be the kind of spouses that reflect and live out the love of Jesus. It is our responsibility to work to win the hearts of our own kids and youth of our church so that they will choose the God that we love. It is our responsibility to live and set a standard that will leave a legacy of true love and purity behind us. It is our responsibility to allow God to make our hearts ready for the soon return to Jesus and to help others be ready for the return of Jesus. It is our responsibility to be a solution to the problem with purity. It's time to be a disciple of the purity of Christ and make disciples. Go Ye Therefore.

ENJOY THESE OTHER TITLES BY AUTHOR DUSTIN HALL

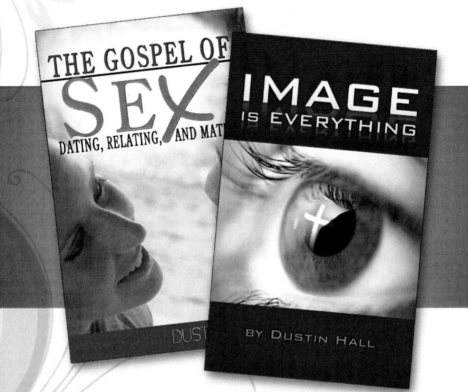

Gospel of Sex Every day, young people are assaulted with sexual imagery and music that pressures them to make unbiblical choices about what they do with their bodies. Thus it is vital to arm you and your family and friends with the tools to fight the battles of sexualized pop culture and peer pressure successfully. And now you can do just that with this brief but powerful book.

Image is Everything Who am I? Where am I going? How do I get there? God made us with thinking minds, and His desire for us is to think, study, and trust Him so that those answers will become readily apparent. This book was prayerfully written to inspire young people to permit God to lead their thinking and submit to His will for their lives.

www.RemnantPublications.com • 800-423-1319
Remnant Publications, Coldwater, MI